Chapter	Table of Contents	Page

Special thank you to Cheryl Workman Underwood of 1972

I0023271

To address and solve problems that were created as a result of colonization, historic subjugation & White Supremacy.

What's the objective?

To stimulate everyone's interest in Fort Wayne History and in solving social problems and issues created due to psychological conditioning. This BOOK is the result of what happens when a few people invest a few dollars to make change.

What is the book about?

This BOOK showcases Blacks who don't feel intimidated because of US History. They boldly discuss their personal motivations behind seeking success, and their attitude mindset of "I can defeat institutional challenges", complete with explanation on how they did it.

Intellectual Consensus

This BOOK contains an intellectual consensus of an age, gender, occupation, skin-shade, and vocational cross-section of Blacks testifying as to how they deal, have dealt with and overcame personal challenges. These industrious, everyday citizens showing signs of success will give hope and

Publisher and HackonomicsTV Talk-Show Host Eric Hackley with granddaughter Keziah

I wanted to write a book for Keziah & other young children to read early in life, about Black people and their overcoming life's challenges. About Blacks being unafraid to speak forthrightly, making positive changes, while contributing to the betterment of all Americans, especially Black people.

a direction to Blacks across America that they too can be united and should support **OPERATION StudentNomics** to rebuild their Black communities through Self-Education.

Please enjoy the many original stories and commentaries of Blacks overcoming issues and adversity. Although different, each story exhibits spirit, heart, love and not being afraid of competition.

KEKIONGA BLACKS' War on HIS-Story & Slave Mentality

OPERATION StudentNomics   p.3

Whether or not you believe Willie Lynch was a real person or is a myth, you have to admit there is tangible evidence of his existence. In fact, the 1712 Willie Lynch letter states that if his plan is not rebutted within 300 years, that a new and evolved SLAVE mindset will be created that will become the basis of a new manufactured mentality that will be representative of the full manifestation of the African Slave being killed, but psychologically broken. If my analysis is correct, what do I propose to do to remedy this situation?

Program Concept: The United Nations of Fort Wayne

My Plan is to use the 1712 Willie Lynch social problem as an educational opportunity for Middle and High School Students to become involved in TV Productions. Selected students will revolutionize the local communications industry in a grassroots historically relevant, social and self-educational way with incentives.

In 2008, I conceived this idea and in 2010, incorporated it into the United Nations of Fort Wayne. The Nations will be in remembrance of Ottawa Chief Pontiac who destroyed Fort Wayne 250 years ago, Shawnee Chief Tecumseh who was killed 200 years ago and Hackley In-law Chief {who killed to most European Terrorists} Little Turtle vs. Hackley In-law George Washington during the **KEKIONGA WARS** of the 1790s. My aim is to create 3 Student TV Production Organizations, separate with no affiliation to any Fort Wayne area School Corporation and Fort Wayne Public Access Television. These Student News Organizations will simultaneously function as vehicles of Fort Wayne History awareness in honor the Native American Chiefs they represent..

All ethnic student members will be encouraged to participate because of their capability to report their perspective on international issues and events. Students will educate their community and themselves through each other's TV shows. Student Productions will feature interviews with non-traditional community leaders. Individual Student Productions will be driven by students themselves, featuring their own talents and personal interests. With the help of sponsors, at the end of the semester or academic school year, an Oscars type of Awards Ceremony with prizes and cash incentives can possibly become a reality. Fort Wayne Middle & HS Students are the conceptual base for a Great Lakes Region Student News Organization Network.

KEKIONGA BLACKS' War on HIS-Story & Slave Mentality

HackonomicsTV

Kicked off Fort Wayne Public Access Television
After 30 years of Talk-Show Productions

Eric Hackley interviews Access TV Station Manager Norman Compton about the
National #1 status of Fort Wayne Public Access Television

Writing a Book is Therapeutic

I decided to write a book after I was kicked off Fort Wayne Public Access Television after 30 years of hosting and producing cable TV Talk-Shows. The 1st thing I want to say about Fort Wayne Public Access TV manager Norman is, he's one helluva nice guy.

Low keyed, stoic, and will listen calmly and patiently to what you have to say or discuss. He's a good manager although, perhaps his company policies that he's choking me with may reap with just a pinch of Historic White Supremacy and Jim Crow.

I had believed that we were partners together in cable Television, to enlighten the world of ethnic people in Fort Wayne. I thought that sharing my goals and objectives would be intelligent, as I viewed him as an ally in pursuit of my and his Public Access

KEKIONGA BLACKS' War on HIS-Story & Slave Mentality

Television destiny. Therefore, I with full clarity of mind, henceforth nominate myself retroactively, "HOUSE Nigger" of the Year 2011.

I confidently thought we were a team until I was kicked off the air after doing a Live Call-In Talk-show with Kevin Muhammad. Norman, like I said is a heckuva nice guy. When he finally wrote me the letter that for months I asked him to write, he did and gave it to me on March 11, 2011. In fact, he was such of a nice guy, that he even read it to me. However, I did inform him that I knew how to read. I guess to help me understand, he took a step physically closer to me and as he read, he used his finger to point at the words as he said them. Boy what a helper he is.

Not being sure of my comprehension level, he wanted to help me to understand. What a guy! Norman's letter said, "your check out privileges at Access Fort Wayne has been suspended since this incident. Despite that, you checked out equipment twice in the month of February, and I have reminded the staff of your suspension. In addition you have asked other AFW volunteers to check out equipment on your behalf circumventing your suspension. These are major violations "A" and "I" of AFW's Operational Policies and cause me to take action.

Violation A: Owing funds to ACCESS FORT WAYNE due to failure to pay for equipment damage,

Violation I: Checking our equipment on behalf of a non-certified producer or for a producer on suspension.

You are banned from using any of Access Fort Wayne's facilities or equipment until the camcorder is paid for. Your studio times have been cancelled. You do have the right to turn in programs to play on the channel but you can not make them using our equipment."

Violations "A and I" in my opinion contain Jim Crow logic traps and debatably tend to favor the Slave Owner or Access Manager's Rule interpretation over the Producer

I knew that sometimes when people think you have a slow temper, they may tend to view that as an exploitable weakness and try to play you. I am most definitely in no way suggesting Norman has racist tendencies because he's such a heckuva nice guy. But I feel he was being a little bit excessive. I asked Norman for 7 months and on numerous occasions for a letter of clarification on my being suspended. It took Norman from July 22, 2010 until March 11, 2011 to give me a letter detailing my suspension. I needed clarity because I smelled a Kangaroo Court on the horizon. And I wasn't exactly sure what a verbal suspension meant. Since I am an innovative person, I tend not to give into obstacles, real and/or man made. Norman and I have experienced conflicts consistently around July 4th and Black History Months as infraction dates indicate. And to compound matters further, It was **NEVER MADE CLEAR** as to what I could do and could not do concerning Fort Wayne Public Access TV equipment.

During this same time period, Michael Patterson, editor for *Frost Illustrated* offered me the opportunity to write for Frost Illustrated. I said yes because I saw an opportunity to sharpen my interviewing and writing skills and the opportunity would help me to momentarily ignore the Fort Wayne Public Access TV issue, but it nevertheless lingered in the back of my mind. By focusing exclusively on writing allowed me the opportunity to think about the possibility of writing a book about Fort Wayne Blacks.

Through Frost Illustrated, I am working diligently to develop my journalistic abilities and showcase inspiring, thought provoking issue-oriented stories of Black people being progressive, instead of perpetuating the statuesque enslavement mentality. And instead of only presenting Fort Wayne Black Innovativeness only on Public Access Television, I can now additionally present my works in *Frost Illustrated* and put their videos on Facebook and You-Tube.

To help me get back on local TV so I can use their "Live Call-In Show" capability and much needed studio, a person offered to have a fund raiser to pay the money that Fort Wayne Access says I owe them because of my "negligence and abuse." I said no, I won't do that because the idea sickened me and it feels like returning back to the plantation and asking to be forgiven for escaping. I'm not comparing Access TV Manager Norman with a Slave Master because he's a helluva nice guy, it just intellectually feels that way after viewing his subjective criterion.

As I was walking through downtown Fort Wayne thinking about why I felt as though I being played with, out of nowhere swooped Melvin Odom on his 10-speed; a friend I've known all my life. He didn't know about the extremely mild depression I was going through, nevertheless, Mel said, "Here, I think you should look at this". He loaned me his *Hidden Colors DVD* and suggested for me to especially be observant of Dr. Francis Cress Welsing.

I did what he suggested. Afterwards, I remembered seeing Dr. Welsing when I was in college on either Donahue or Tony Brown or both. I enjoyed her soft spoken style and laser tongue as she articulated her theory of Racism/White Supremacy. In her discussion, she mentioned a guy named Neely Fuller Jr. I researched Dr. Fuller, called him and he actually answered his phone. He and I have spoken twice and if I can get to Washington, DC, I will give a 110% effort to secure a personal interview with him. I was recently listening to the Washington, DC based Carl Nelson Show (09-24-2013) on YouTube featuring Dr. Neely Fuller. In this fairly recent discussion on Racism/White Supremacy, it seemed as though Dr. Fuller was speaking directly to me.

Dr. Fuller said, *"Everybody has problems. People will talk about their problems. But when you start trying to talk about solving a problem without talking about racism, you're not really talking about solving the problem. Now that's what people need to be aware of. Because that's what people have been deceived into believing, that there are other problems out here that you can solve and you can't be bothered with racism because you've got to solve these other problems.*

But what they can't see, because of the deception and because the racists have been very deceptive to perfection, they're perfectionists when it comes to deception. They say people will not even recognize racism when they see it. And they will be chasing all around trying to solve all these different problems that they say they have, when the main problem they have is the problem of racism which stands in the way of them solving all the other problems they say they have to get to.

That's why I have it on the back of my book. It says, no major problem can be solved in any area of activity, economics, education, entertainment, labor, law, politics, religion, sex, and war unless you address and actually solve the problem of racism. You're going to keep having all these problems, I don't care what your problem is, if you are classified as non-white and you're on this planet. If you're anywhere on this planet, you better be thinking about solving the problem of racism or every problem that you have, you have, you're going to continue to have it."

In conclusion, I found Dr. Fuller's commentary most enlightening, emancipating, and therapeutic.

Rick Stevenson
Wayne Township
Trustee, 320 E. Supe-
rior St., 449-7000

Mike Gaston
TURN' N HEADZ
Barber Shop, 4234 So.
Calhoun St., 744-3069

Scott Williams
Jesse & Son's Barber
Shop, 1401 Hanna St.
(260) 422-5931

Jonathan C. Ray
FW Urban League
2135 S. Hanna St.
(260) 745-3100

The Scope of
KEKIONGA BLACK THINK~TANK
is to be a
History Community Asset,
Cultural Resource
and Visionary Catalyst
for the Framers of
Fort Wayne &
Indiana Propaganda,
and the awakening of our
citizenry to its *hidden* history

Bob Hawkins
House of Fish
2619 Weisser Park
Ave. (260) 456-2040

Ebbie Clark
& Sons Auto Clinic
1921 So. Harrison St.
(260) 498-0277

Donovan Coley
CEO, FW Rescue Mis
-ion, 301 W. Superior
St., (260) 426-7357

Jesse Booker
Commander Amer.
Legion Post 148, 705
E. Lewis St. 423-4751

Edward N. Smith
Atty, Frost Illustrated,
3121 So. Calhoun St.,
(260) 745-0552

Sheryl & Bennie Edwards
Presidents of the MLK Club. Inc
(260) 760-6867
bjecsm011@verizon.net

Lewis H. Griffin
GRIFFIN LAW FIRM
202 W. Berry St.
(260) 426-0242

I would like to sincerely thank Eddie Russell, Larry Chapman, Gloria & Albert Smith, Rev. Bennie York and other professionals, citizens, disabled & laborers who were willing to work with me on numerous Black Community educational projects for the past 30 years.

Larry Chapman
Chapman
Auto Diagnostic
Service,
1137 Eliza St.,
(260) 420-9494

Gloria & Albert Smith
Butch's Exhaust
3501 Winter St.
(260) 745-7547

Linda Brooks

Pinkie & Ola Irby

Melvin Odom

Rev. Bennie & Velma York, Trinity House of Hope Half-Way House 3028 Bowser Ave. (260) 745-7830

Kenny Stevenson

Bianca & Noah James Woods

Robert Carpenter

Rose: Contracting, Complete Home Repair, Siding, Concrete, Kitchen (260) 433-4051

Eddie Russell

Anthony J. Ridley

Ray Russell

Ray Mack, Owner **Madea's** Soul Food Place 2006 S. Hanna St. (260) 444-4933

Edward Young a.k.a. Elder Yonah Hbs Computer Networks **(260)220-2921**

Queen Nefertiti Williams

Scooter & Preonda Rouse

Bridget Williams-Whitt

Carlos Townsend *Premium Cuts BARBERSHOP* 3530 So. Calhoun (260) 804-1982

Jerrell Ward & Ollie Harvey

Donald Clark

Rev. Isaac Fincher Jr.

Anthony Washington *PRECISION CUTS BARBER SHOP* 7504 S. Kmart Pl. 220-4016

Great, great, gr.
Grandmother
Martha Lindsey
{1830 - 1923}

Great, great
Grandmother
Lizzie Lindsey
{1850 - 1933}

Great Grand-
mother Belle
Patterson Lyons
{1870 - 1949}

Married 75 Years

Grandfather
P.A. Lyons Sr.
{1891 - 1986}

Grandmother
Jessie Lyons
{1894 - 1990}

Linda Stanley
Genealogist

This Book is dedicated to the remembrance of our

AFRICAN ROOTS

Salute to my Mother

Even though my parents were divorced, my mom always showed enthusiasm for my visiting and desire in building Hackley family relationships. She always displayed interest in my research and curiosity.

Hilda Lyons Hackley
{1927 –2001}

Anytime my father wanted to take me to Michigan, for any occasion, it was never a problem. She expressed as much love and compassion about Hackleys as my great aunt Virginia expressed about the Lyons family. Aunt Virginia always would ask about my mom's family with true love and interest. She too motivated my interest in Roots.

Cletus Edmonds
{1945 - 1999}

Eric & Aunt Marcelle Lyons
French at her 90th Birthday party

(Chad) Cletus Edmonds III & mom **Gail Edmonds, Linda Stanley** & **son Alan** and daughter Angela and Rhea Edmonds Kaiser (Offspring of Cletus Edmonds).
Keziah is looking over the shoulder of mom **Erica**, granddaughter & daughter of Eric Hackley

KEKIONGA BLACKS' War on HIS-Story & Slave Mentality

Introduction to the HISTORY of HACKLEY Genealogy

Erica w/Lidietty, 1st Cousin and guardian of Sandra's Children.

Sandra's daughters **Jaylene** born 2003 and **Juliandra** b. 1997, with Erica. My father would have been proud to know these three beautiful young women, his grandchildren.

Daughter Erica attending Juliandra's Sweet 16th Birthday Party Celebration

Peggy Forbes, 1st Black woman to start a Money Management Firm on Wall Street

MISSION POSSIBLE: The purpose of the John William Hackley Clan of Hackleys is to stimulate all Hackleys interest in American history and why it is important to connect our individual family segments to our larger national family genealogy.

My plan is to interview Black, White and Miami Indian Hackleys from across America because we should all theoretically have the same DNA, unique history perspectives, motivations and orientations. With your help, we will write and create an original Chapter of United States, England and African History.

Lisa Powell - Calif. Civil Rights Leader

John Woodford
Noted Editor

Michelle Ware Dancer,
Daughter of Virginia Hackley

Gary Mayberry
Hackley Traditions

Narada Michael Walden
Won 1988 & '93 Grammys

KEKIONGA BLACKS' War on HIS-Story & Slave Mentality

How I Became Interested in Fort Wayne History

To answer the question of how I became interested in history, you will need to accompany me on a journey that began many years ago, during my junior year at Elmhurst High School. A life altering moment happened one day in my US History class that was being taught by Mr. Robert Passwater. During one particular class, Mr. Passwater warned me about being disruptive in class. I responded back to him in a direct fashion and he relocated me and my desk into the hall for the next few days. As I had to sit in the hall for an entire hour each day I was kicked out of class, I began to get bored and for some reason, I began curiously looking through my US History book, beginning with the name index as I looked for the name Hackley. I found the name Richard Hakluyt. I looked at the name Hakluyt and knowing how American names morphed as they evolved from Old English to the American version, I said to myself, it looks like Hackley to me, so as I started reading about Hakluyt in the very beginning pages of the my US History book.

As years went by, I discovered that the name Hakluyt did turn into Hackley as evidenced in a book, "The Life and Times of Charles Henry Hackley. His Hackley genealogy shows the spelling changes of De Hackluite, Hakluyt and other variations in route to Hackley from the 1400s to 1600s. Richard Hakluyt {1552-1606} taught Cosmology at Oxford University, was known as a chief promoter of American Colonization. He created propaganda to persuade Queen Elizabeth to financially back his and Sir Walter Raleigh's plans to plant a Colony at Roanoke in 1584. This venture became known in history as the "Lost Colony" and all the people froze to death waiting for supplies from England. Although Hakluyt never visited America, his name appears on the 1606 Virginia Colony Charter. I created Hackonomics in remembrance of Hakluyt.

The first of my branch of English Hackleys to be born in Virginia was John Hackley in 1655. In 1691, he and his wife Elizabeth Boulware had a son, James, born in 1691. James and his wife Elizabeth Shippy Hackley had a son John, who was born about 1716 in Essex Co., Virginia. John and his wife Judith Ball Hackley were married on March 16, 1734. President George Washington had family relationship with the Hackleys of Virginia because his mom, Mary Ball Washington was first cousin to Judith Ball Hackley.

KEKIONGA BLACKS' War on HIS-Story & Slave Mentality

Richard Hakluyt {1552 -1606}	Geo. Washington {1732 -1799}	Capt. James Hackley Jr. {1790 -1826}	Capt. Wm Wells {1770 -1812}	Chief Little Turtle {1752 -1812}

Jerome Hackley {1846 –1917}	Albert Hackley {born in 1880}	Don Hackley {1901-1955}	Charles Hackley {1927-2000} and dau. Sandra {1973-2010}	Eric/daughter Erica Bryant

John and Judith had many sons, but for the purpose of this essay, I will only focus on two of them: Captain James Hackley Sr., born {November 11, 1751} in King George Co., Virginia and his older brother Francis. Captain Hackley Sr. fought in the Revolutionary War in 1776 under George Washington. In fact, many other Hackleys fought under George Washington at this time of our history. Capt. James Hackley Sr.'s son, Capt. James Hackley Jr. was born April 11, 1790. This is the Capt. James Hackley Jr. who married Rebecca, the daughter of William Wells and granddaughter of Chief Little Turtle. William Wells, at 12 years old was kidnapped and raised by the Miami and assumed the Indian name of Apekonit of the Miami, eventually married the daughter of Miami Chief Little Turtle. Wells fought along side of Little Turtle at Harmar's defeat and St. Clair's defeat.

Dennis Neary wrote and produced "*Three Rivers in Time*", a documentary that said William Wells scalped so many Americans at the 1791 St. Clair's defeat that he couldn't raise his right arm. When Anthony Wayne joined the Little Turtle Wars in 1794, the first thing Wayne did was to hire William Wells, made him Indian Agent and gave him the rank of Captain. William Wells became employed by the American Army. At the 1794 Battle at Fallen Timbers, Wells fought against the same Indians that he had fought with against the Americans in earlier battles. The Potawatomi never forgave Wells, calling him a traitor. They finally caught up with Wells 18 years later on August 15, 1812. The Pottawatomi shot William Wells the chest, scalped him, broke open his rib cage and pulled his heart out and ate it. William Wells, again is the Father-in-law of Captain James Hackley Jr.

Captain James Hackley Sr.'s older brother Francis, {1740 - Oct. 21, 1817}, is buried in Franklin County, Kentucky. Francis at 50 years old, had a sexual relationship or encounter with an African slave and produced a daughter who carried the name Francis Hackley, born in 1790 in Culpeper, Virginia. Francis became the mother of John William (Billy) Hackley, born in 1807. Francis (the African offspring) is my great, great, great, great grandmother and she and Captain James Hackley Jr. were biological first cousins.

John William Hackley and wife Ann became the parents of 16 children. Their youngest son was Jerome I. Hackley born free in Niles, Michigan, 1849. Jerome is the father of Albert, born 1880. Albert is the father of Donald Hackley, born 1901. Donald is the father of Charles M. Hackley {1927-2000}, born in Kalamazoo, Michigan and Charles M. is the father of me and Sandra Hackley. Sandra has 2 daughters, Jaylene Amber Rodriguez and Juliandra Marie Pena. My daughter is Erica and granddaughter is Keziah. From Keziah to John Hackley spans 11 generations and 257 years. So John Hackley of 1655, the grandfather of brothers Capt. James Sr. and brother Francis Hackley, is my great, great, great, great, great, great, great, great grandfather.

What this means is that after the enforcement of President Andrew Jackson's 1830 Indian Removal Act that was applied in Indiana in 1846 to herd the Indians out of Indiana, there are Hackley Miami Indians (the offspring of Capt. Hackley Jr. and Rebecca) scattered from Indiana to Kansas and Oklahoma and I would like to connect with them. These are the offspring of Chief Little Turtle and William Wells lineage. These Miami Indian Hackleys and I should have the same DNA and I want to test the accuracy of my research. If any of you know any Hackley Miami Indians locally or in Kansas or Oklahoma, please ask them to contact me at hackonomicstv@gmail.com or at frostIllustrated.com.

The irony here is that George Washington died in December of 1799, Little Turtle and William Wells died in 1812 and Captain James Hackley Jr. and Rebecca weren't married until 1817 after everyone had died. The interesting point is that Hackleys were present at the kick-off of the 1500s English Colonization of the Americas movement from Richard Hakluyt to Chief Little Turtle, grandfather of a Hackley who was the first to sign the 1795

Treaty of Greenville giving the United States to all the key ports of the Great Lakes Region of America. The Kekionga War history gives Blacks metaphoric insights into the War on Willie Lynch.

Therefore in conclusion, my advice to high school students is, when you're kicked out of class for being disruptive and you're sitting in the school hall with nothing to do, explore your text book. You might be surprised at what you may discover.

Erica recently said to me that I was the only Hackley she knew and she knew nothing about our history. Therefore I took her and Keziah on a 486 year journey thru Hackley history and genealogy, bridging us with and from Englishman Richard Hakluyt {1552-1616} to Keziah, born in 2008.

KEKIONGA BLACKS' War on HIS-Story & Slave Mentality

Questions Ignored by Fort Wayne Educators, HIS-Storians & Downtown Elite

Revolutionary War & Battle at Fallen Timbers Hero Major General Anthony Wayne

3 Key Questions:

What did Anthony Wayne do to:

(1). Warrant a Statue constructed in his likeness?

(2). Have a City named in his honor?

(3). What if Anthony Wayne would have lost the Battle at Fallen Timbers?

Everyone who knows that Fort Wayne was named in honor of Anthony Wayne gets an "A" in Fort Wayne HIS-Story. However, I have observed that any knowledge beyond that, the only thing most people know is how to spell his name, and that's about it.

Anthony Wayne was one hell of a glory seeking leader, with "Balls of Brass." Mr. Wayne came into a situation where all previous generals who went up against Chief Little Turtle were either killed, severely disgraced to the point of resignation from the army, or became the answers to American history trivia questions.

Anthony Wayne was on a potential suicide mission. But that was the mindset of our American Mentality leaders. The American leaders of this era knew that if they kill in large enough quantities, they could become president. Can you imagine if the Indians were a football team who defeated and destroyed three different European teams, one French team led by Calvary Officer Augustin Mottin de LaBalme and 2 Euro-Americans who were formerly British led by Josiah Harmar and Arthur St. Clair, where all 3 teams were defeated by 50-0? The necessary attitude to overcome an obstacle of this magnitude is where the metaphors for sports and war collide where winning and losing means life and death.

But Anthony Wayne figured out a strategy and defeated the Indian coalition so that the United States of America could take control the land so that it could eventually be sold to European immigrants at a 100% mark-up. They would sell land to anyone except Black people. Anthony Wayne's mission was primarily the same as his predecessors, to kill the Indians and destroy their crops so they would have no food for the winter months. But Wayne's focus had to be on defeating Chief Little Turtle because he was the main nemesis of George Washington. Little Turtle caused President Washington major headaches and embarrassment especially in front of Congress, thus resulting in the first usage of Executive Privilege.

But the thought and idea of only focusing on Anthony Wayne during the Anthony Wayne Statue Removal jibber-jabber debates accelerated in January, 2013, reads like a distorted fairytale. You can't logically mention or discuss Fort Wayne history or Anthony Wayne without equally mentioning Chief Little Turtle. If you do so in any context, you're authoring HIS-Story, an agenda-driven propaganda filled re-fabrication of local American history.

During the entire eight month jibber-jabber debate period between the Fort Wayne Mayor, City Council, Allen County Public Library, National Parks Department, local historians and citizens surveyed at random, everything was centered around European esthetics and the cost of moving the Statue. A library official boasted about the plaques of Little Turtle and Tecumseh that are presently displayed on the wall in their genealogy department. To me, that just doesn't feel right. The only thing missing in this picture is a Black Lawn Jockey and the Frito Bandito being pictured next to these heroic Native Americans. If both Little Turtle and Tecumseh had prominent statues in the library plaza, that would be a lot less patronizing.

When the Federal Parks department threatened to revoke the National Park Status of the Courthouse Green if any statues were placed on it, citing that it would ruin the integrity of the landscape, well that's a case of the tail wagging the dog. In my opinion, placing the statues of Anthony Wayne and Little Turtle side-by-side had the potential of shining a national spotlight on downtown Fort Wayne. And for the people who said that putting Wayne's statue on the Courthouse Green would open the door for other groups wanting to place statues there, that's non-filtered, pure jibber-jabber. Who else could possibly deserve a spot on the Courthouse Green besides Anthony Wayne, Little Turtle, Tecumseh or Pontiac? No one except for perhaps Dr. Martin Luther King, and a beautiful bridge had already been dedicated to his memory. If you notice, I keep mentioning Anthony Wayne and Little Turtle in tandem because they were warrior equals. Anthony Wayne came here to kill Indians in the Kekionga Region and Little Turtle killed the most Euro-Americans in US history. You can't get anymore equal than that. But lets not forget that when he died in 1812, Chief Little Turtle was buried with full American Military Honors and to be as far as I can find, never formally honored again by the leadership of Fort Wayne.

Have you ever asked yourself what would have happened if Anthony Wayne would have lost the Battle at Fallen Timbers? In all likelihood, the western border of the United States would probably be in the Toledo, Ohio vicinity. If the Natives would have defeated the Anthony Wayne Euro-Americans, the British would have loved that. They would have immediately seized the opportunity to someway further destroy the Euro-Americans and then the Indians, but not the Blacks. They were still needed for free labor. The French may have had a chance to attack and defeat the Euro-Americans or perhaps the British, but they had to still be in pain from the whipping of Toussaint L'Ouverture (the Black Napoleon), Jean-Jacques Dessalines and the Haitian Revolution. We don't hear much about the Haitian Revolution in conjunction with the Little Turtle Wars of the 1790s and how they took place at the same time. Just think how much confidence that would have given those enslaved Africans if they knew that European powers could be defeated.

Finally, I encourage everyone to read the 1795 Treaty of Greenville. After the Native Americans lost the 1794 Battle at Fallen Timbers, they signed away downtown Chicago, Detroit, Toledo, Cleveland, Lower Sandusky, Maumee including most of Ohio, Kekionga (the 3 rivers) and whatever had a port and access to water because of the international trade and the rich resources of this region of the continent. In return, the Native Americans got $20,000 of value, not in cash or gold, but in blankets, utensils and live stock. Of course, the Euro-Americans assigned the value to the items in trade. Sounds like the making of a fair trade to me, a little bit like sharecropping economics, but with a twist.

KEKIONGA BLACKS' War on HIS-Story & Slave Mentality

Fort Wayne History Perspective by John Dickmeyer

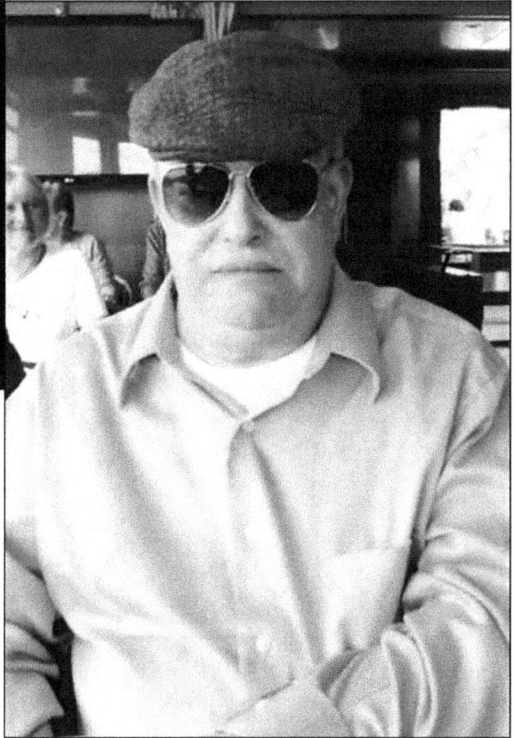

Eric, You are too kind in characterizing the "Miami Removal" to Kansas. It was the 19th Century equivalent of what the Gestapo did to Jews, Gypsies, and any individuals who they wanted to disappear. The 19th century attitude toward diversity was "if it does not conform to Christian protestant moral and social values," we must make it disappear from our communities.

The poor and indigent Miami on the government dole was the "scourge" and "blight" on Northern Indiana. This was the same attitude which worked against immigrants and African Americans. These folks railed against slavery, but wanted the free slaves to settle somewhere else, please.

This is also the same attitude that stole Indian children from reservations to Indian schools to program them to a new culture. All of America needs to confirm to the ideal. It has morphed into the social welfare philosophy of the 20th century, where the social worker has become the arbiter of individual and family values.

By the way, slavery, even when done up in its very best dress, is a vile and abominable practice. It soddens both master and slave, and taints any society which embraces or attempts to justify it. If we deny the true events of history, we work to extend the curse of the evil deeds which our ancestors perpetrated; if we fail to acknowledge the good which they accomplished, we deny to ourselves the blessings which they worked for us as a legacy for our own lifetime and the countless lifetimes of our descendants.

KEKIONGA BLACKS' War on HIS-Story & Slave Mentality

Indiana and Texas Politicians
by Eric Donald Hackley

Hackley encouraging others to speak out and express their insights on today's reality

The only state of political leaders better at re-writing history than those in Texas, are ours located in Indiana. Texas has only totally reframed slavery when equating it with being an unpaid Interns. Indiana on the other hand, has literally deleted Indians from Indiana history and out of Indiana public school education curriculum. According to many dictionaries, the definition of Indiana is "Land of the Indians." When was the last time you asked where are the Indians? What happened to them? Can the same thing happen to Blacks?

I bet if you switch Texas State Legislators with Indiana State Legislators, the people of each state wouldn't notice the difference. Either Texas and Indiana are the same State, or they have taken the art of re-writing history to a Shakespearean level.

Over the past many years, on this specific point is where many Fort Wayne African Americans want to argue with me. Some say that I address Indian's problems too much and I don't put my full focus on Black people's issues. This dilemma makes me contemplate the question, is it easier to interest Fort Wayne

Blacks in TEXAS REVISIONIST HISTORY concerning enslaved Blacks? Or is it easier to interest Fort Wayne's Blacks in INDIANA REVISIONIST HISTORY concerning Indians of Kekionga?

This Fort Wayne story is the reality of how Indians who once lived on this land had it all taken away from them. Then they were escorted off this land to Kansas and Oklahoma to be forgotten about and never ever to be heard from again or mentioned. Revisionary historians constantly change and reprogram us in how we feel, felt, think, not to think, which way to step and how high to jump concerning the issue of Blacks and Indians being involved in the shaping of Fort Wayne History.

KEKIONGA BLACKS are here to offer stimulation and direction to those who fail to recognize that Fort Wayne's Black Community and our rich Native American heritage should be the nucleus of a new Fort Wayne *racial healing* program; designed to open the minds of the many students and citizens who think history is boring and irrelevant to their lives.

Ladies and gentlemen in this instance, it's the same divide and conquer DISENFRANCHISING game being played on Texas and Indiana communities. But many of my Black detractors are too narrow minded to see it. Many of us have mastered the art of keeping ourselves divided and conquered from potential local allies.

KEKIONGA BLACKS are a SWAT team of Fort Wayne Blacks who have a warrior spirit that permeates through a strong, bond and respect for their own African Heritage and culture. And at the same time, they have developed an intense curiosity and respect for heritage and culture of the land on which they now live, and for the people who once lived here who today's local history shows them as being irrelevant, extinct and not at all.

KEKIONGA BLACKS are visionary activists, who through an American history lens see a spiritual connection between the Indians who fought in Little Turtle's Wars against European terrorists and the Black Freedom Fighters against slavery of the same time period through presently. Just as our African history before, during, and after emancipation has been obscured, minimized, changed and ignored; so has the history of Native Americans who occupied this land called Fort Wayne been minimized, ignored and constantly re-edited before our very eyes. And very few citizens especially educators says a thing.

KEKIONGA BLACKS have therefore theorized that the

motivating forces and common denominator between Chief Little Turtle's historic War coalitions of the 1700s and today's Black activist mindset seeking solutions to Black empowerment is the ethnically delegitimizing and debilitating doctrine of early American Racism, also known as historic White Supremacy.

KEKIONGA BLACKS further theorize that the psychological disease known as indoctrinated "Slave Mentality", has led to another psychosis that is very seldom ever discussed. More than 400 years of White Supremacy/Black inferiority ideologies have led to a myopic intellectual sterility, no longer capable of producing real brilliance. Instead of being innovative and truth seeking, it is easier to just change the story and keep the people ignorant. If you keep the people ignorant to facts, you will be able to speak pure "jibber-jabber" with an occasional "quack-quack" and the people will never know the difference.

According to the on-line urban dictionary the "his" in history refers to the White man's story.

For the past eight and a half months, in my home town we've heard enough HIS-Story to be legally certified as retarded in Fort Wayne history. How can you ever discuss Anthony Wayne's name without giving Miami War Chief Little his earned and due respect. Throughout this debate period, no one ever explained: Who was Major General Anthony Wayne? What did Anthony Wayne do to warrant having a statue sculpted in his likeness? What did he do to be remembered by having a city being named in his honor?

Concerning the debate on relocating the Anthony Wayne Statue to the Allen County Courthouse Green, I was in complete agreement with Mayor Tom Henry with one exception, he didn't go far enough. The Statue of Chief Little Turtle should have been included in the deal. The idea of Anthony Wayne and Little Turtle standing side by side would have an educational potential of renaissance proportions. Again, how can you discuss any aspect of Major General Anthony Wayne without giving at least an honorable mention to Chief Little Turtle? How? You just do it in the guise of HIS-Story. Being that the history of Little Turtle's Wars and his biographic history is not specifically taught in Fort Wayne or Indiana schools, we have been voluntarily mis-educated, programmed to be history illiterate and incapable of independent critical thinking.

KEKIONGA BLACKS' War on HIS-Story & Slave Mentality

Love Is The True LIBERATOR

Chief Condra Ridley

At Eric's request, I am really thankful for this opportunity to be with you. I really enjoyed listening to all the different speakers and hearing the various stories. I think we're very blessed in America because we have so many important and enriching stories from the various people who have come to inhabit this land. To the Miami Chief, I give honor to you and your people. I was moved by your music and your drum. I recognize from my own cultural background that the drum represents the heart beat and I'm really moved and touched by that.

I'm really grateful today to have the opportunity to be a part of this movement to clarify and if need be, rewrite Fort Wayne history. We are now really blessed in this community to have so many people who have come to inhabit this land of Fort Wayne that was once called Kekionga.

When the Chief mentioned that Columbus in 1492 discovered America, well that's when someone else tells their own story as if the world began when they were born. How foolish is that?

Eric asked me to come here today to share a particular song. Today I'm also involved in the Black Expo because I'm always taking part in cultural and educational programs concerning the Black community. I have a book I brought along with me today because I am a student of true history because I like to know the truth. And I know the truth will set you free.

This book is titled, "Ain't Gonna Let Nobody Turn Me 'round." It's about a song you may have heard during the civil rights struggle. This book is about stories and songs of the Civil Rights Movement. Civil Rights are important to me and Human Rights are even more important. There's a poem that I want to share with you. This is written by Margaret Walker, an African American writer and poet. She wrote this poem that is titled, "For My People" and I think it's very important for us to reflect on these words.

KEKIONGA BLACKS' War on HIS-Story & Slave Mentality

Since we know America is a nation of immigrants, everyone came here from somewhere else, except for the Native Americans. I know this is your land and I'm thankful of the opportunity to be here on this land especially now, being of African descent. We've had a challenging story too in the "home of the brave and they say, the land of the free." But we haven't always been free here.

Margaret Walker said in her poem "For My People," "let a new earth arise. Let another world be born. Let a Bloody peace be written in the sky. Let a second generation full of courage, issue forth, let a people loving freedom come to growth. Let a beauty full of healing a strength of final clinching be the pulsing in our spirits and our blood. Let the martial songs be written, let the dirges disappear. Let a race of men now rise and take control. I hope that nation of men means women rising too. Let us all come together in courage, unity and love, because love is the true liberator.

Richard and Chief Condra Ridley

KEKIONGA BLACKS' War on HIS-Story & Slave Mentality

Local Insight into the Redskins Issue

Interview with Chief Brian Buchanan, Miami Nation of Indians of the State of Indiana

Hackley: Why did the "Savage and Redskins" name stick to Native Americans?

Buchanan: Several names have stuck. I've even been approached by Channel 15 News. There's a lot of things history has done to demean Native Americans in general, not just the Miami.

What we choose to fight, we have to pick our battles. We have to pick the battles we know we can win. Just because it's immorally incorrect doesn't mean we're going to win. I learned this from the North Side Redskins situation. Channel 15 came to me and asked what I thought about the name Redskins? I'll tell you, it's a derogatory name. I'll say it again, It's a derogatory name. I had another 20 minute interview with them. What's the Tribe going to do about it? The name of North Side High School is over 80 years old.

Right now we've got more important things to do with our people. We are so dispersed with the diversity of our own people, we've still got that going on. It's not bad, but it's diversity. We're not going to choose that fight. That school was named North Side Redskins a long time ago. I don't like it and I'm sure there's a lot of other Native Americans who don't like it. But that's not a fight we've chosen to go after right now.

When you tell people why, do you want to be called Blackskins? Or Yellowskins? No! It's not right. So when will the morality of society come to the level of saying, it's not right? Let them fix it on their own. We didn't put it out there and they know how we feel about it. But I'm not going to fight them on it.

Hackley: That's where you need an independent entity to come in who enjoys fighting like we do.

Chief Brian Buchanan: You're good at that Eric.

Hackley: That's where the commonality lies among the different ethnic groups. Because ethnic groups are all focused on other issues that are immediately more important to them that they let battles like this Redskins Issue lie dormant.

Interview with Brother Kevin Muhammad, Nation of Islam

Brother Kevin Muhammad: Columbus was trying to find a new land. The truth is that he wanted to find a new route to India. But he got lost in his navigation from Europe to India. When he got to this land, he thought he had arrived in India. So the people who he saw that were already here, he called them Indians. So today, we call the Native Americans, Indians.

I would not agree with you in saying that his travels should be blamed on Muslims, but you mentioned his navigation. What the Europeans wanted was, since they were dissatisfied with their government in Europe, they wanted to set up a new government. But they knew that they could not do it in Europe so they wanted to find a new land to set up a new government that would satisfy their dissatisfaction in Europe. So they found a new land and people on that land. But they wanted and needed to get the people off the land, to take control of the land to set up this new government that we now call the United States of America.

So no brother Eric, it was not the fault of the Muslims. The Muslims ousted the Europeans out of many parts of Africa and the Middle East because there was trouble making going on in Africa by the Europeans and they could not do trading with Africans. They did not want the European influence in the conquests of Africa so they made them go in another direction, so they were forced to find another route to India.

KEKIONGA BLACKS' War on HIS-Story & Slave Mentality

The route they chose landed Columbus in the Americas.

Hackley: Since Columbus headed in this direction to find a route to India, one could make the argument that the United States should have been called Indiana.

Kevin Muhammad: I agree with you brother. If you want to call certain parts Kekionga or name certain things Miami, Seminole, credit should have been given to the people who were already here.

Hackley: When are we going to create a real and true identity of Fort Wayne?

Kevin Muhammad: Fort Wayne to me is a very divine place. I love the way you continuously reiterate the Native American influence on this land. It's a very sacred place to me right here in little bitty old Fort Wayne in the state of Indiana. We have to move past arrogance, we have to move past ignorance of the true history of this land where we are so that we can grow and advance. Chief Little Turtle made great contributions to this land and to the struggle of his people.

But again, I say that the arrogance to think that not only Native Americans, but darker people in general are insignificant. So we can move them out of the picture to try to get control of the natural resources of this particular land. That's what this was all about.

There was heavy, heavy fur trading that was taking place on this land and the Europeans wanted a piece of the pie, a piece of the money and a piece of the wealth. How do we get into the fur trade?

Now instead of fur trade, it's drug trade and trafficking. How do we get a piece of this money? Well, we have to take control. We have to break up the unity. We have to put one person against the other and try to take control. It was the same thing that happened then. This was a great trading route because of the Three Rivers. This was a very wealthy part of the country in the 1800s, 1700, and 1600s.

So as a thug would think, how can I get a piece of that? So a plan and plot was put together about how to take control of this land. And the arrogance is that the darker people who are there are insignificant and are less than the Europeans. Therefore in the minds of the Europeans, their actions of destroying and manipulating the original owners of this land for profit were justified.

KEKIONGA BLACKS' War on HIS-Story & Slave Mentality

Terry Doran, Talk Show Host/ Producer of Theatre for Ideas

Hackley: Terry, you wrote a Journal Gazette editorial a few years ago talking about how you wanted to change the name of Fort Wayne back to Kekionga. It was titled, "City's name a painful reminder."

Terry Doran: Yes, I said Fort Wayne was not a very nice name for a modern city. It was named after a man whose main claim to fame was violence, who was sent here by George Washington to kill people. I still think it's a disgraceful name for a city."

Hackley: Weren't you worried that Fort Wayne people would become outraged and would organize themselves to run you out of here? Because it seems like we're not very intellectually open to hearing discussions like ours.

Terry Doran: You're right. In addition to writing editorials like that one, around the same time, I did a "Theatre for Ideas Show" called "What's in a Name, Let's Change Fort Wayne." Not a lot of people showed up, but I remember that people were sort of aghast like, "why would you change the name of our city?"

Hackley: Perhaps there is a conspiracy. I recently I attended the Peru, Indiana 164th anniversary of the of the Miami being boated out of here on the Wabash River to Kansas and Oklahoma. That was the execution of President Andrew Jackson's 1830 Indian Removal Act. The only politician there was the Mayor of Peru. There were no other political dignitaries, educators or student groups present. At a time when we're only talking about improving our test scores, there has to be a score for general intelligence and local history literacy?

Terry Doran: I like that! These standardized tests (ISTEP), you frequently see how student scores fluctuate, but you don't see anything on the validity of these tests. What are they testing? In the testing, they certainly miss a lot of important things. This gets us back to the point of why we're talking about local history.

KEKIONGA BLACKS' War on HIS-Story & Slave Mentality

Local history is not talked about. If it's taught in school, they're discussing how quaint the Indians are and look at their neat moccasins. Or you can go to powwows and see all the things they make, but very little about the history.

Hackley: I use to attend multi-cultural meetings at IPFW. One of the ethnic members created a culturally safe game where you match the ethnic face to the style of dress and the country. As I sat back and listened to the concept behind this game, this multi-ethnic body (headed by a Caucasian) wanted to play a modern day version of pin the tail on the donkey.

Knowing that we have real issues going on in the world, there was nothing about how in most cases each ethnic group representative had a lot in common with Blacks and Native Americans, which is why they were here in America today. Most of them did not come to the United States on vacation and decided to stay, US soldiers rescued them because of their government in someway trying to kill or starve them. Just like early American history.

Terry: I wish I had the answer to why so many Americans were like this. I've done so many shows and it's hard to get people to come to them.

Hackley: I'm not suggesting that people are like that because of a lack of interest in local history, but I have come to the conclusion that they don't know the history because it is watered down and the schools don't sell it. In 2008, I was informed by an Indiana educator of how Indiana Public Schools had re-edited its text history books. They are no longer required to mention Indians when they teach Indiana or US History.

The reason you can't get Fort Wayne people to a local TV-show about Fort Wayne history is their relation to local history is about the same as American's relationship is to Chinese arithmetic. The Indiana education corporations have deleted (Indian and Kekionga History) the only common denominator between today and the past.

By our local and state Public School Corporations ignoring the history of Kekionga and we as Fort Wayne citizens all sit idly by, unaware as to what's going on, we have become systematically conditioned accomplices to our own local history illiteracy. Consequently, trying to stimulate interest in local history within the Fort Wayne community is similar to urinating in a stiff wind where all your effort blows back in your face.

KEKIONGA BLACKS' War on HIS-Story & Slave Mentality

Open Letter Commentary
Responding to the Doctor's Inquiry

Dr. Carl Lee Whitt recently expressed an observation on my face-book page. Dr. Whitt postulates, "Black businesses in Fort have a big problem with trust. It is difficult to help each other when we don't really want to see improvement in another person's well being.

Dr. Carl Lee Whitt
KEKIONGA BLACKS' War on HIS-Story & Slave Mentality

First of all, I agree whole heartedly with Dr. Whitt. But I don't think he went far enough into a scientific analysis. Too many Blacks say that Willie Lynch is a myth and doesn't exist because they haven't seen a birth certificate, or no early Black icons ever discussed him and because many of the words and phrases used in the "Final Call" newspaper version of the Willie Lynch letter, "Let's Make a Slave" were not yet in existence. But if it looks like a duck, walks like a duck and quacks like a duck, it's Willie Lynch.

I agree there is a psychological dilemma facing Fort Wayne Blacks that no one seems to want to directly and forthrightly address. A possible reason for this reluctance is contained within the "perceived-risk" of publically looking like you don't like White people. So therefore, you distance yourself from initiatives, especially if the traditional Black players are not in the forefront or at its conceptual nucleus.

But the {wanna-be negro elite and aristocracy} can't be in the forefront, because of their fear of offending White people {and their grant money}. Therefore traditional Black leadership is in a social, psychological and economic Catch 22. But to avoid wasting time and spewing meaningless rhetoric aimed to enlighten the perpetuators of local HIS-Story and their slave mentality accomplices, we Kekionga Blacks feel that declaring War is the only answer to this paradox.

In February, 2012 and coincidentally the 300th Anniversary of 1712 Willie Lynch, I created a calendar to officially "Declare war on Slave Mentality" and to stop the nonsense of how we Blacks are destroying each other through the way we have been behaviorally conditioned, psychologically indoctrinated and socially played. Consequently, I lost about half my support for the calendar project that was titled *"Fort Wayne Blacks Declare War on Willie Lynch Slave Mentality."* Many felt I was a little too assertive and did not in any way want to be portrayed as possibly acknowledging or confronting the existence of historic White supremacy.

For the February, 2013 Calendar, I hustled and replaced those cowardly Blacks, and ideologically separated myself from them. That's when and why I created the concept of Kekionga Blacks. Kekionga Blacks are African Americans who have a strong knowledge and pride of their own African heritage. But they also have the wisdom and curiosity to know the importance of being aware of the history and heritage of the land where they now reside.

KEKIONGA BLACKS' War on HIS-Story & Slave Mentality

On the February 2013 calendar, the theme was Fort Wayne HIS-Story Reform, where we Kekionga Blacks saluted three of the greatest Indian White Supremacy Fighters in the history of the history of the United States of America. The calendar recognized the 250th anniversary of Chief Pontiac's Rebellion in Fort Wayne on May 27, 1763. On the same date, May 27, 2013, nothing was mentioned by the local media and leaders.

The calendar recognized Chief Little Turtle's July 14, 1812 {201-year memorial} of his death from natural causes. I naively thought that on his death bicentennial, the Fort Wayne Politicians, Educators and HIS-Storians would surely recognize this war hero. I was wrong again. Perhaps I was a bit over optimistic in accessing our leader's desire to be inclusive in telling the history story of our city. But the fact is, the Indians of the Indiana Territory who killed the most European terrorists in US history, have been made to become extinct, courtesy of Indiana politicians, Public School Educators and Fort Wayne Community historians. They have collectively, and I'm sure unintentionally, successfully erased the Indians from our consciousness of our landscape right in front of our faces; therefore making the legends of local Shawnee, Miami and Pottawattamie Indians extinct and in their eyes, historically irrelevant.

Can Blacks be erased from our consciousness just as easily? I don't know the answer to that question. Call a Texas or Indiana Conservative. They will know, they've done it.

History can be used as a tool for understanding any conflict. Ignoring local history does not change the facts. And yes, I do feel our local history is uniquely situated to give us specific insights into the core of American HIS-Story and the Willie Lynch quandary.

So, Dr. Whitt, thank you for your inquiry. Sometimes thought-provoking questions create thought-provoking answers. In conclusion, the issues of self-regenerating slave mentality and Fort Wayne history illiteracy have got to be dealt with at some point in time and that time is now.

We Kekionga Blacks have adopted a War strategy that was successfully implemented in the Little Turtle Wars of 1790 and 1791. The War tactic of using rifles, knives and arrows to kill European Terrorists, metaphorically can be translated and used by Blacks. But instead of killing terrorists, we use Black people's personal interviews of dealing with adversity to kill Willie Lynch. Tell me where I'm wrong!

KEKIONGA BLACKS' War on HIS-Story & Slave Mentality

Opening Consciousness Receptors through Rap History

Facebook conversation with
Alan Eric Stanley of Indianapolis, In

INQUIRY: The Historic Impact of Run DMC

Alan Stanley: I had this on VHS back in the day. I probably watched this a hundred times. I think you recorded this for me when I was about 18 years old.

Hackley: Most interesting. This is direct evidence of why we need to open our Black history receptors. When you look back at that era's social conditions that influenced Run DMCs innovativeness, we are in that same historic cycle loop today. But because of Federal Grants, Tradition oriented Leadership, HIS-Story Indoctrination and Willie Lynch Slave Mentality, generations of Blacks have become behaviorally programmed and convinced that anything about history is boring, having no relevance in their daily lives. Consequently, we have become perpetual victims of Willie Lynch Slave Mentality due to our willingness to ignore the origin of socio-economic conditions that motivated the genius of Run DMC yesterday and others today.

To remember 28 years ago with such precision is interesting. Run DMC must have captured a certain essence of the mid-1980s Black psyche. For those who were too young or those who didn't see the social relevance of Run DMC, would you please enlighten us as to what Run DMC did that impacted Blacks during their time on top. I know that they did. I just can't articulate it.

Alan Stanley: If you remember when MTV first came out, they really only played rock music. There was not much diversity in the musicians video's played on MTV. The only black artist that received regular rotation was Michael Jackson because of "Beat It and Billie Jean". They played "Rock Box" by Run DMC (a single from their first album) every now and then. When Run DMC's second album came out they released "King of Rock" as a single (that was also the name of the album).

KEKIONGA BLACKS' War on HIS-Story & Slave Mentality

MTV put that video into somewhat regular rotation. When they re-leased the third album in 1986 (Raising Hell) a song called "Walk This Way" was the second single released. That song received heavy rotation and made it to #1 on the MTV charts. That broad-ened the audience for Run DMC and rap music as a whole. and rap music as a whole.

You started hearing Run DMC on white stations during drive time. Prior to that, rap music only was played as Chuck D from Public Enemy said, "in the mix late in the night". Because of the success and popularity of "Walk This Way" and "Fight for Your Right to Party" by the Beastie Boys, MTV started a show called "Yo MTV Raps". I think Run DMC hosted the very first show while they were on the "Tougher Than Leather" Tour.

That show opened the door for numerous new rap groups. The show stayed on until around 1994. MTV took it off because they basically felt it was not needed any longer. Rap music was dominating their programming at that point. In a nutshell, Run DMC took rap music to the "suburbs" and made it mainstream. A good book to read on Rap/Hip Hop music is "The Big Payback - The History of the Business of Hip-Hop" by Dan Charnas. It takes you from the beginning to about 2010.

Hackley: Congratulations to Alan for completing his college edu-cation in his 40s. And yes, he's still a fan of Rap/Hip-Hop music.

Alan, thank you for this important history input.

Dad Gary, Alan, mom Linda and
sister Angela Stanley at Alan's college graduation

KEKIONGA BLACKS' War on HIS-Story & Slave Mentality

RUBIN BROWN:
A 1960s Mississippi Voter Rights & Central HS Student Activist

Tina Bristow Cohill & Rubin Brown at Hana Stith's 85th Birthday Party

What was it like growing up and being socialized in Biloxi, Mississippi in the early 1960s?

Rubin Brown (RB): It was like in any other city where you knew your place. We lived in the negro/colored concentrated section of town which started at the railroad tracks and went over to Biloxi Bay. Biloxi in surrounded by water on 3 sides. Blacks knew to go to the back door and to say yes mam and no mam regardless of the age of the White person. You could go to the Greyhound Bus Station to get a meal, but you had to eat on the colored side or you had to eat outside.

How did Blacks feel about that. Were they upset? Or did they just go along with the program?

(RB): They had no other alternative. To do anything less meant putting our life in jeopardy.

Who fought for your rights and against the injustices?

(RB): The NAACP did one on the most radical things ever when they tried to integrate the beach which was 26 miles of public area. Blacks could fish in the Gulf of Mexico, but weren't allowed to swim in the water. But we swam there anyway. As long as there was only 2 or 3 of us, Whites wouldn't say anything. But if it was 10 or 15 of us, that's a different story.

How did you become involved in the Civil Rights Movement?

(RB): My mom had joined the NAACP in 1960 or 61. The president of our NAACP, Mr. Gilbert Mason, was also a member of my church. He was one of the most prominent doctors in town and was the Boy Scout Troop leader. He was a Jackson State graduate and went to Howard University Medical School. He was an interesting man who knew his history always spoke about Black history to us.

But it was Mr. Hatchett who really turned me on to Black history. His sister was secretary of our church and I knew her very well. She was also a disciplinary 6th grade teacher. But Mr. Hatchett was a drunk. He had fought in WWII and the Korean conflict. He was an older man who lived around the corner from us. I would always see him staggering home drunk from being out drinking. One day I decided to mess with him. I said, Hatchett, you're drunk and he said yes and you're dumb. Now I got offended.

I told him he was drunk and dumb. He said, I know something and you don't know anything. I said, what do you know that I need to know? He said, "you don't know anything about your history." I answered, Black people don't have a history. He said, "that's what I'm saying, you're dumb." Hatchett said, "you don't know who Hiram Revels is. He was the first Black Senator from Mississippi." I just about lost it. I said, I know you're lying now! A Black man has never been senator of Mississippi. He said, "like I said, you're dumb", and he staggered on home. The next day I went to school and found a book by Langston Hughes entitled, "A Pictorial History of the Negro in America" and discovered Mr. Hatchett was right. I read the entire book when I was in the 3rd or

4th grade and that's what started my quest into reading about Black history. I discovered a whole new view of Black folks. We had been something! We had power and successes!

Then I had the opportunity to hear the NAACP National President Roy Wilkins speak when he came to Biloxi. His speech was about celebrating 100 years of emancipation, yet we're not free. He really fired me up as he spoke about reconstruction, segregation, school desegregation and all the obstacles that were put in our path to keep us ignorant, dumb and in poor jobs. Wilkins made it all fit together in an understandable way.

Shortly thereafter, I saw a flier that directed me to another meeting that was not too far from my house and Fannie Lou Hamer was going to be there. It was about a summer project of 1964 where they were going to organize each county in Mississippi with the goal of registering Black people to vote.

Voting was the most important thing a Black person could do in a state that probably had the lowest turnout of Blacks with the highest percentage of Blacks in the population. The NAACP, CORE, SCLC and SNCC had joined forces and were working together on this project to register people to vote. They chose Mississippi as the 1st test site because Blacks were 60% of the population.

What was your role as a young kid?
(RB): At first I was passing out fliers but later I said that I wanted to learn how to register people to vote. So they put me with a team and I was to listen and take notes and then I really started to enjoy it. My first scary encounter happened across the bay in Ocean Springs, Mississippi where my team was to canvass the area, hand out fliers, promote our mass rallies and register people to vote

Then the Chief of Police showed up and told us that we had to stop what we're doing. So I challenged him and the Chief said, "boy, I'll put your butt in jail." So I laughed at him. He said, do you have five dollars? I said no. "I should arrest you for vagrancy." I said, you can't arrest a minor for vagrancy, I'm 14. He didn't believe me.

I was the only one of my group to get censored because I quoted what I thought was a bible verse to him, "Those who say they love the lord but mistreat his fellow man is a lie and the truth is not in him." He got upset and asked me. "Are you calling me a liar?" I said yes I am. I felt confident that nothing would happen to me because a crowd started to form, but I did get scared when he took me to the fire station because I knew it was for a butt whipping. Several of the White kids who I was working with followed us down there. He asked again, "how old are you?" I showed him my work permit. He said, "Boy, get out of here and take your butt back to Biloxi."

The 1960s were an awakening. There is a song we sang: We are not afraid today, and before I'll be a slave I'll be buried in my grave, going home to my Lord and be free." We literally believed that. And to see a room full of young people with that same mentality is something we had never seen before.

After Rubin Brown's mom died, he moved to Fort Wayne to live with relatives and brought the mentality of organizing Blacks to fight injustice with him.

After leaving Mississippi, Rubin Brown became President of (BSSC) Black Society for Social Change and led the 1968 Central High School Black Student Walk-out in 1968, 45 years ago.

1968 Black Student Walk-out
Rubin Brown & William Tubbs Muhammad

Rubin, what inspired your Black Community activism?
(RB): 1964 was a pivotal year for me. I worked as part of (SNCC) Student Non-Violent Coordinating Committee Voter Registration in Biloxi, Mississippi. This is at the time of Fannie Lou Hamer's poignant stance of wanting to register to vote in probably the most backward state in the nation, and the deaths of Schwarner, Goodman and Chaney. We were surrounded by the students who came for the Mississippi Freedom Summer, that plus the blessings from my mother who was the acting secretary of the Biloxi NAACP is where my impetus came from.

Muhammad, what inspired you?
William Muhammad (WM): In 1968, when both Rubin and I were high school juniors, the only history education we had was HIS-Story, about George Washington, the Cherry Tree and honest Abe. But about revolution, we didn't find out until later that it meant bloodshed, and we didn't want to shed any blood unless we necessarily had to. My main motivators were the Black Panthers and Malcolm X. Malcolm's Ballet or the Bullet use to get me fired up and ready for battle.

What made us think we could make a change? We were

**Interview with President Rubin Brown and VP William Tubbs Muhammad
of the 1968 {BSSC} Black Society for Social Change**

getting ready to go to Viet Nam supposedly to fight and give our lives for our country. I took a page from Muhammad Ali's, "ain't no Viet Cong ever called nigga." So I wasn't going anyplace to fight an enemy way across the pond. My enemy was right here in the State of Indiana, in the Republic of America. So what drove us was the fact that we really believed that we could make a change.

Some of our mentors really helped us like Nate Norman, Dave Miller, Jackie Patterson, Elizabeth Dobynes, Charles Redd, Tom Brown, to mention a few. Some of our elders were, Coteal Walton, Albert Bruener. We felt that once the BSSC got together and started formulating ideas, it led to a lot of awakening like who we were and being proud to be Black. I didn't like the word negro back then and I don't like the name African American now. It's just my personal choice. You'll never be an American. You live within the geographical region of America, but your origin is from Mother Africa.

How did your idea of having a student walk-out develop?
(WM): It was two things. We got wind that Central might be closing in a couple of years and there was a march over the opening of new schools. The idea was that they would close Central and open Northrop and Wayne. We wondered, why would you close a perfectly good school and open schools way out in the country

where Caucasians live?

There was a lot of interracial dating going on at the time. A Central football player slapped a White girl and one of our football coaches said, "We ought to hang him." We always got little snipes of things like that. Racially, we knew where we stood. One time at a Weisser Park Junior High student dance, we attempted to merge Black and White students. One of our teachers came out waving his arms, "get back, get back. White students over here, Black students over there". Now this was in the mid 1960s. At Central, interracial dating was called "scene fighting."

Then, there was the Ministerial Alliance. This is not a knock on them, but the late Rev. Dr. Jesse White was a community activist. We called him "The White man's mouthpiece." As a matter of fact, preachers period, whenever the Black natives got restless, the Ministerial Alliance was always sent in. "Alright now, ya'll calm down now." Well we weren't going for the okeydoke anymore.

When we came to Central, the Black to White student ratio was about 60% Black. At the time of graduation, it had reversed to where Black students were numerically dominant. They called us "the minority majority. "Brother Rubin Brown, Joseph Timberlake, Lawrence Williams, Charles Van Pelt, Dennis Walton, Charles Myatt, William Patterson, Sue Hassell Stubbs, Janice Magee, Beverly Stalling, Coteal Walton and myself were members of the BSSC. We desired a Black History Club, Black teachers and we wanted a Black History course to be taught to the student body.

We also wanted a Black guidance counselor. Robert Horstmeyer was the Dean of Boys. Just imagine a young Black student wanting guidance and college information and what a 1960s White man would tell you about your career choices.

What was your key concern?
(RB): The administration was omitting us. Central was 60% Black at the time. There was nothing that acknowledged that Central was predominantly Black. It was like they didn't want it to be known. In essence our culture was being suppressed. Not only was it done in our face, it was down right wrong. We decided to bring this out. Not only did we have an Art Festival, but we had speakers who came in and spoke to us. Bob Starke who was an excellent Artist was one of our speakers.

The Dean of Boys asked, "who put you all up to this?" No one put us up to this. We CAN think! We had meetings for about a year where we had speakers, we would listen to albums and we read all kinds of books. Our spirit emanated from a lot of places.

(WM): It was just like we caught a cold, we caught the flu.

And they actually asked, who put you up to this?
(WM): The school administration didn't think we were independent enough to be able to think on our own. They thought we were influenced by "outside agitators." We did have a couple of teachers on our side. One was a sister named Queen Brame. She put her personal life on the line. Her fiancé threatened her. I'm paraphrasing but he said that "if she got involved with those militant students, their engagement would have to be postponed." It was real drama. From my way of thinking, they felt we were getting input from the Urban League.

How did Malcolm X influence your thinking?
(RB): Malcolm was the first person to really come out and say, "hey, things in America is all backwards". We're either going to have to vote or fight and the gun will be our weapon.

Philosophically and conceptually, it sounds like you were implementing in the BSSC what Malcolm X was saying. How did the walk-out idea start to galvanize?
(RB): The walkout idea developed over the year during our meetings. As we continued to meet, talk and share our views and we kept reading. William Patterson especially read a lot and would always talk about Malcolm and the movement and it was interesting. Not only was it interesting, my coming from Mississippi, I knew what the deal was. The bright lights of Fort Wayne was kind of camouflaging the real deal. We were still poor. We were still the worst and most hated people in America. No one ever saw the abuse of our neighborhoods, the abuse of our parents and that's what Malcolm was talking about and we wanted to change that.

Was it offensive for you to be called a Black Militant?
(WM): For me personally, it was a badge of honor. Leading up to the walkout, we presented a list of ideas to the school administration of what we wanted. They weren't demands, they were requests. We wanted a Black history Club, a black Guidance Counselor and a Black History course to be taught to the student body. Their answer to us was NO! So we walked out!

After they said no, we had a series of meetings at the Urban League and at each other's homes. We used the meetings for strategy sessions, to tweak our ideas and to keep the fire burning. In our school curriculum we wanted to hear more than just

George Washington and honest Abe. We wanted to hear about Toussaint L'Ouverture, Jean-Jacques Dessalines, Nat Turner and Denmark Vesey. Now those guys were heroes. Back then, I was in a mental zone and didn't realize it. I was hypnotized by Malcolm in one ear and serious brothers and sisters in the other. It was like reality TV.

According to the doctrine of Willie Lynch, when Blacks have secret meetings, usually there's one Black who can't wait to tell authorities, did that ever happen?
(WM): Oh no! We didn't play that! We didn't have any Uncle Toms in our group. If we did, he was real low profile. I don't think we had one of them. None of our plans were ever leaked because they would head us off at the pass anyway. In fact, they knew what we were going to do. But they didn't believe we would go through with it. They thought we were hot heads just blowing smoke.

MORNING
OF THE WALK~OUT

(RB): Early that morning Principal Paul Spuller collared us and said, "you know if you all go through with this, you can't come back to Central." **William Tubbs Muhammad** said "Spuller threatened us and we don't play that!"

(RB): We had already made our plans. Their threat was humungous and we called their bluff. "You all do what you have to do and we're going to do what we have to do, and we did it".

The morning of the pep session, at a certain time, we were going to walk-out of the school. During the pep session, Rubin nudged me. Tubbs are you going? I said, man, we're supposed to. He asked me again. Are we going? Are we going? All of the sudden Rubin stood up. I stood up. Brother Patterson and the rest got up and headed to the Lewis St. entrance. We didn't realize how many students had joined us. A total of 65 students walked-out that day. We wound up getting suspended for 3 days.

In RETROSPECT by William Tubbs Muhammad

With Allah God as my witness, do not be ashamed, do not be afraid of the truth. The truth will set you free, a lie will continue to make you a slave. I'm proud of the fact that I came through this period of time which tested my metal, my grit and I have no regrets about going through the 1960s.

KEKIONGA BLACKS' War on HIS-Story & Slave Mentality

What I'm most proud about is a little bit of organization skills a couple of high school students had. The most Honorable Elijah Muhammad said, "Unity for a Black Man is as powerful as an atom bomb". I will leave this with our current generation. It's in your hands, continue to carry it on. If you need to know something, ask those who went through it.

By Rubin Brown

It was an experience that we shared. Even some of the people who I run into now, we still talk about it. We were very proud that we did it and I think some good things came out of it.

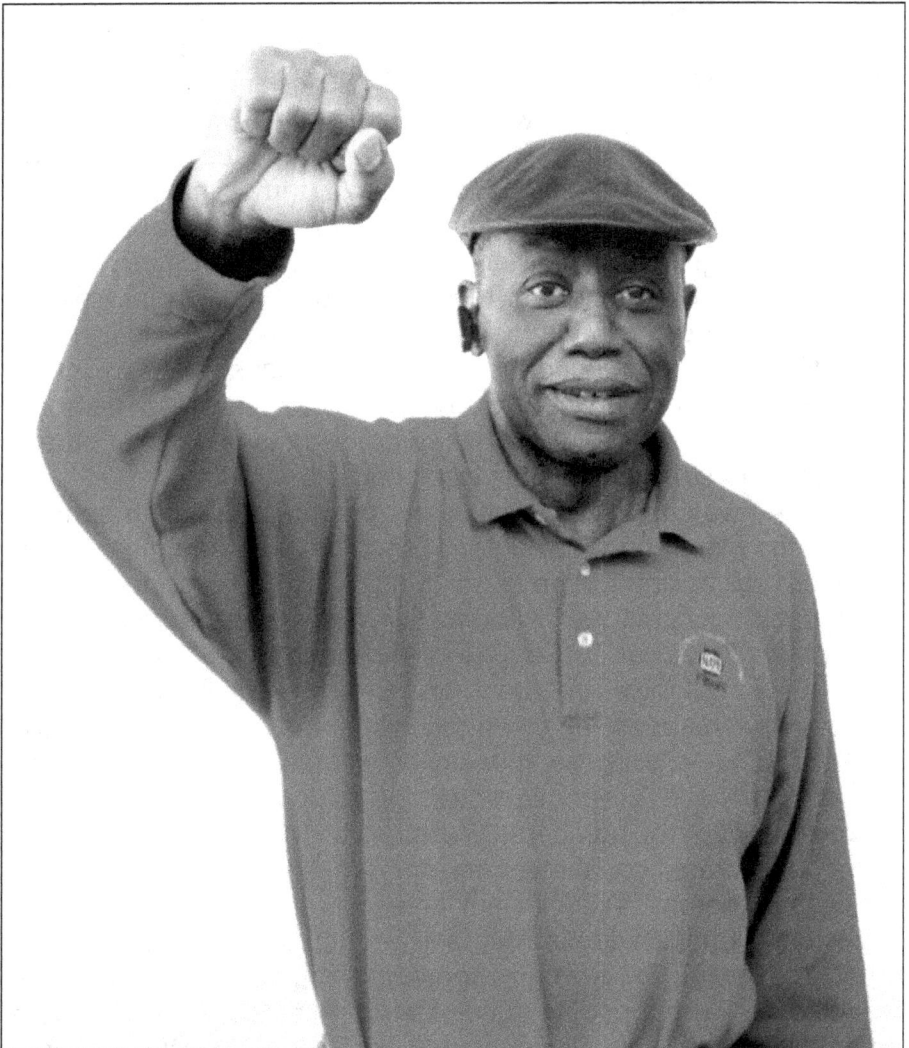

Rubin Brown with 1960s Black Power Salute

KEKIONGA BLACKS' War on HIS-Story & Slave Mentality

I Can't Understand This Country Anymore

Juanita White received a BA from Yale University and has done post graduate work at Memphis State University.

I grew up with so much hope-for my future, for my children's future. It was right on the tail end of the civil rights movement, in the shadows of Dr. King's death and smack dab in the middle of Watergate. Things had to get better because the country was facing - and had faced - some dark times.

Fast forward now, some forty odd years later. What on earth has happened? Politicians want to control what happens in a woman's womb. Check. Talk of repealing Roe vs. Wade. Check. (Impossible I would think, but who knows?) Supreme Court struck down a section of the Voting Rights Act, allowing for states, mostly in the South, to change election laws without federal approval. So that means the big bully state of Texas immediately put a voter identification law into effect, and announced that redistricting maps would no longer need federal approval. Here we go. There will inevitably be some marginalizing of black voters into some districts and out of others, making it more difficult to elect black officials.

As I watched the festivities surrounding the fiftieth anniversary of the March on Washington, I became more and more angry. We were still asking for the same things King and Company asked for in 1963-economic parity and justice. Will we still march and beg in another fifty years? Will things ever change?

They will if we, the Black and Brown and colored people in the country, the poor and disenfranchised, the haves and the have not's, decide to exercise the power we have. Indeed we have power. We have economic power. We have voting power. We have the power of numbers. We must become a more sophisticated electorate, consumer, citizen. We have power over who goes to Congress. We can put pressure on these officials-once elected-to nominate those men and women to the bench who will apply the law justly. We can choose to shop where we will be respected and where people of color will be hired, or we can choose to not shop there, exercising the power of our purse. We can make a difference. Will we?

KEKIONGA BLACKS' War on HIS-Story & Slave Mentality

I can remember Cletus Edmonds saying over 50 years ago in referring to Archie's jump shot, "Boy, that guy could see."

50th Anniversary of the 1963 North Side vs. FW Central HS Fight

Richard Stevenson, Velvet Van Pelt Brooks and Archie Smith

I would like to put the past 50 years into perspective. You all graduated Central High School during the Civil Rights Movement and during the time of the March on Washington.

What are your earliest memories of one another?

(Richard Stevenson Sr.): I don't remember not knowing Archie. Archie and I go back to the late 1940s. We were childhood friends at McCulloch Elementary School. Then in the early 1950s I met Velvet. Velvet and I have been friends so long that we are family more so than friends. She knows my family. We go to church together and we've been socially acquainted for a long time. As a matter of fact when I reflect back to my Harmar Junior High basketball days, Velvet was one of the outstanding cheerleaders. She has been a friend and a personal cheerleader for a long time.

(Velvet Brooks): I don't remember Archie early on, but Trustee Stevenson, I can remember back to Harmar School. From GAA

KEKIONGA BLACKS' War on HIS-Story & Slave Mentality

(Girls Athletic Association) to running track, playing basketball and high jumping. We do go way back. My mother is connected with his family. We still attend Pilgrim Baptist Church, and we're involved in a lot of the same things. I know Archie from his being popular in high school basketball.

(Archie Smith): Rick and I had formative years at the McCulloch Center. We played basketball together. In fact, when I first began playing basketball, every time I took a shot, he would block it. So he kind of helped me develop my game. I knew Velvet from High School. I remember her from the McCulloch Center dances that we used to have.

Is there much of a difference between today's Black community and yours in the 1960s?
(RS): There is a lot of difference. When we were all young, we knew each other in one way or another. When Velvet said she knew Archie because of his popularity and Archie said he had seen her a lot of times at the McCulloch Center, now called Jennings Recreation Center, was a common ground for all Blacks and we magnetized there. Most of us from back in the day, if we didn't know each other by name; we knew each other when we saw one another.

Differences among individuals were resolved much differently than they are today. Instead of a shooting, you may have a fist fight with someone, but afterwards you became the closest of friends. There were no animosities that would linger on that would perpetuate hostilities toward one another. As a matter of fact, Velvet I can remember when we were all small that no one had a lock on their door. But now, and it didn't happen overnight, most homes have three or four locks on their doors.

You mean that when fights happened, the issue was dealt with and when it was over, it was done with. Just like that?
(AS): Most of us knew each other. If you had a problem, sometimes your parents would get involved. They would bring the kids together and sit down and talk with them. I remember when we were kids, Billy Files and I would fight almost every day. I remember once he broke my glasses and I took them home to my dad and we were talking about it. He said, "I'll tell you what we'll do. We'll go over and talk with his family." So his father and my father started talking about it and the next thing you know, Billy and I became the best of friends. That's how things were resolved then. It

wasn't like I'll lay back and wait for him and get him later. It just didn't happen like that.

(RS): Archie, wasn't your first car a 1955 Pontiac?

(AS): Yes it was.

(RS): Boy that was a cool car back then. I say that because now days just about every kid and their sister and brother have cars. Cars among kids were a rarity back then. The way we got around was by walking or on a bicycle. Even though we lived within walking distance, often we were not allowed to go more than three or four blocks away from home. And because of that, as Velvet was living in the Madison and Hanna Street area and Archie and I were living on Hayden and Eliza Streets, I really didn't start socializing with Velvet until I got to junior high school because we were four or five blocks away from each other.

But the school districts had their boundaries situated where Archie and I went to McCulloch and Velvet went to Harmar. And at the time, McCulloch was a predominantly White school with really very few Black students. And just a few blocks away was Harmar, that was predominantly Black. We didn't get the experience of being around a lot of Blacks in school until we got to the 7th grade.

What was your mindset at Harmar that made you such great athletes?
(VB): A lot of it, I think you were born with. But we had boundaries and we had to stay within that radius of where we lived. That meant we played with the same kids and we practiced all the time because that's what we did. We didn't have bikes at that time to ride; so instead, we built our own pole vault, made our own volleyball nets and the alley behind our houses was our track for running relays. So with all that practice and God given talent, that helped us a lot right there. We had some good athletes that came from Harmar.

(AS): We didn't go out just to become athletes. We liked sports and we liked a lot of different things. But as far as basketball and football was concerned, we looked up to some of the older guys who played sports. Naturally when we were younger, we had heroes we wanted to be like. We had John Kelso and Johnny Bright and these were outstanding athletes. We also had Bobby Milton (who for 34 years, was well known as a player, coach and an Ambassador of the Harlem Globetrotters). There was also Mr. Al Jennings, who we didn't even know was a great athlete and blanket winner from Central. We always saw the older man, but he was a heck of an athlete.

Why is it that anytime Central athletes did anything great, Fort Wayne Blacks felt good about themselves?

(AS): That's because Central was the only Black high school in our area. The majority of the Blacks at Central fed in from the inner city. The majority of Blacks went to McCulloch, Harmar, James Smart, Adams and Hanna Schools and they all fed into Central. That's why everyone in the Black community showed pride in what we were doing.

Did the teachers at Central care about your academic success in the 1960s?

(RS): One of the things that was unique in my situation, even at an early age when I was at McCulloch, I saw the significance of education and I strived to be the best that I could be even back then. That stayed with me when I went to Harmar. At the time we had X, Y, Z and ZZ lanes for students. X lane students being intellectually the smartest. I always strived to be in the X lane, a couple of times I found myself in Y lane classes. As I went to Central, I did the same thing.

My mother wanted me to do well academically, but it was something within me that wanted it, too. I took the hard subjects, algebra, geometry, trigonometry, physics, and chemistry because I just had that within me of wanting to know. In other cases at Central, they had industrial classes for those who were interested in mechanics so that they could pursue that because all of us are different. Everyone didn't look at academics as I did. Some liked working on cars. Some liked to weld, draw, and paint. And some of the pretty girls liked the business classes and were studying to be secretaries or were interested in bookkeeping. But I was happy with my education at Central and even today, I'll put my education up against anyone's education.

Velvet, you just retired from being an educator. Were you pushed at a young age?

(VB): I'm in agreement with Rick, the need for an education was instilled in me from home. I can remember when we were leaving Harmar, getting ready to go to Central is where the preparation started. As I said, my parents were strict on this and we had just each other. Before I got to Central, I can remember in my last year at Harmar in the 8th grade, that Herb and Nate Banks sat next to me in class. We had a teacher who said, "I came to teach. Those who want it, sit over here. Those who don't, sit over here." I was totally stunned that there were kids who did not want to learn. The teacher never failed a student. He was an excellent teacher. But the kids who did not want to learn could put their heads down, but just do not disturb the others.

Did some kids actually put their heads down and sleep?

(VB): Oh yes. This happens here, there and everywhere, it is nothing new. When I was going to Central, I don't think I was thinking about going to college. I was thinking more about the monetary side, how my family would be able to afford my going to college. So I wasn't thinking about college. I was thinking on another level to get into something else. I can remember going to my counselor and asking about this. No counselor ever said to me that I would make an excellent doctor or lawyer. I'm not sure how I could have done it, but I never had one of them push me into that area. I remember speaking with my mother about this and she said, "You can be anything and do anything you want to do with the help of God."

I was offered a job at the last of my sophomore year, which kids didn't usually get until their junior year, at Lincoln Life. I had the opportunity to get this job as a sophomore. An attorney called and told me they wanted to hire me that summer to work. My last name fooled them. I remember walking into the office, not for an interview because I had already been hired through school but no one had met me there. I remember walking in for my appointment and was waiting to sign the papers for employment. The secretary said, "We have one person coming before you." I said ok, but it kind of stunned me because I knew this was my appointment time. Something made me ask the secretary if the person coming was from my school because the only two schools involved were Central and South Side. She said, "Miss Van Pelt should be here now." I said, I am Miss Van Pelt. That experience kind of changed my thinking of what I wanted to do and how I wanted to do it. I got the job and could have worked for them later in life.

Just a moment. How did the secretary handle it when you told her who you were?

(VB): She apologized and said she was so sorry. But I knew what the jest of it was. She looked at "Van Pelt" and expected another face which was ok. I was used to that.

KEKIONGA BLACKS' War on HIS-Story & Slave Mentality

(RS): Back in the day Velvet, if you were a Smith or a Stevenson they probably would have presumed you were Black. But very few Blacks had names like Van Pelt and Velvet. I can understand that. Even today when I hear some of the names of Black people, I might think to myself, that doesn't sound like a Black name. You can't go by the names anymore to distinguish anyone's ethnic background, but back in our early childhood, you could.

(AS): When you look at the names today's kids are giving their children, they are hampering them. The "Sheniqua's" and so forth. You can name your child what you want, but you do have to think of the consequences down the road.

How were the relationships between the Black and White students, since Whites were the predominant group?
Speaking for myself coming from McCulloch School, we had a lot of White friends. And we had some White friends at Harmar too. Being involved with sports, you're around all ethnic groups. So we didn't really have any problems. The majority of us got along well. There were some flare-ups naturally, but the majority of the kids at Central got along well. We still had our cliques, though. We ran in certain groups and others ran in their groups.

What about interracial dating?
That was a "no no", but it happened. They frowned on it and didn't like it. If you were caught taking a young Caucasian lady home or downtown and the police stopped you, you'd probably go to jail.

Seriously?
(AS): Yes.

(RS): Archie, I don't think any of the athletes during our time dated White girls. I know you didn't, I didn't, and Cletus Edmonds didn't. Preston Underwood and Jimmy Martin didn't. But it was a common thing. Many of the young people who were our age as you know, many of them ended up going to Boy's School, because they got caught dating White girls and their parents were not fond of that. They were good people, but they ended up going to Boy's School. If they were a little older, they would have had a felony behind their name. Often the term "Statutory Rape" was used. I'm glad they didn't bother our Black girls too much back then.

　　　　One thing I can say about back then, we Blacks in Fort Wayne had not absorbed the spirit in other cities where Blacks were being more progressive, and we got a little complacent. Even though we could go to school with Whites and could disagree with them, we still knew our place. And our place was Eliza St., Hayden St., Madison St., and we had limitations. You would not go into White areas of the city. You would see them in school and would not fight with them, but they had certain enjoyments that we were not exposed to. How many of us were exposed to high school drama? How involved were you in their special clubs in high school? We didn't get involved in those things. All of our social activities were centered around the McCulloch Center.

With that being your reality, how did the social conditions not hamper your self-confidence?
(VB): It all comes from home. First, I had a strong mother and father. I kind of knew what I wanted to do at an early age. I didn't want to work for anyone, that's why I started out in business for myself until I started my family. I think in being a female, and having a strong father figure at home, which the kids don't have a lot of that today, no one could tell me anything that my mother and father had not already instilled in me from home. So I think it made me a little more sure of what I was, what I could do and I wasn't afraid to take a chance. I wasn't afraid to step out there and go beyond the boundaries. But I think in being a female, I wasn't exposed to things most of the males would have seen. In talking to Archie earlier, he was telling me about a section of town he was very familiar with. In 5th or 6th grade, I would not have known anything about that. I never rode a bike.

McCulloch Center was our world. In school, I was in the Republican Club. I don't know how I fit in because there were 19 in that group and there were two Blacks. So in being girls, we just got along better. Not that we didn't get upset with one another about different things that were going on, we handled it differently.

At that time weren't most Blacks Republicans?
(RS): They were called Lincoln Republicans. There might be a few Lincoln Republicans around today. They were called Lincoln Republicans because, as we know from history, Abraham Lincoln was the president responsible for freeing the slaves. So Blacks clung to the Republican Party for a long time. If you go back and study history, you'll find it was the Democratic Party that was against civil rights and voting rights and it was the Republicans who were supporting those issues. It kind of flip flopped when President Roosevelt came on the scene and later on John F. Kennedy and President Lyndon Johnson.

KEKIONGA BLACKS' War on HIS-Story & Slave Mentality

You go back and look at Frederick Douglas when he said, "It's a poor Black man that would ever vote as a Democrat." That's changed now because you get a bad feeling if someone is Black and Republican. That's a way of saying how far we have come because we all have individual rights and freedom of opinions.

Wasn't that at the time when Malcolm X called Democrats White Supremacists?

Yes.

(AS): The power of the Democratic Party was in the south. Today, the reason most Blacks won't vote Republican is because the then Democratic Party, hijacked the today's Republican Party. The southern Democrats were called Dixiecrats. These Democrats moved over to the Republican Party because of the civil rights movement and when President Johnson signed the Civil Rights Act, the Dixiecrats hijacked the Republican Party. That's why we have the problems today with Republicans. When you say today's Republicans are radical people, look where they came from. They came from the Dixiecrats of the south.

Were all 1960s Blacks considered Black Militants?

(AS): If you raised your voice toward someone and said you can't do this to me or my people or if you said going in the back door is wrong, you were a radical. If you had a voice of your own to say this is what you believe in, what you're doing to me is wrong, you were a radical.

How did you not let that social norm detour your freedom of expression?

(RS): I think Velvet answered it best when she said, the home setting. Our parents, like most parents in the 1940s and 50s, wanted better opportunities for their children. They taught us our morals at home. Way before there was a Martin Luther King talking about non-violence, our parents taught us about turning the other cheek, doing what was right and to resolve issues by ways other than fighting. It was instilled in us to become overcomers before we had the opportunity.

As time went by, we saw and we knew that it was time for a change and it was time for us to step up and say what was right and what was wrong. In times past, we just took it and went forward. I'm so glad, Archie, that things are no longer like when we were playing ball because we were limited to McCulloch Center. If there was a basketball game in a public park two or three blocks away, we knew not to go over there because that was the White people's area and we were not welcome. But I'm glad that things are different today.

Velvet, do you know I have a grandson and he's number one in his class and has been for about five years in Fishers, Indiana, the White suburban part of Indianapolis. His dad is an attorney and his mom is a school teacher. I said he should be a successful student. He lives in a $500,000 home and this kid, Archie, doesn't know his best friend is a White girl. He doesn't have the baggage that we have. All he knows is that she's his best friend. He doesn't realize she is White and a girl. He's just out there in a middle income area doing the best he can, socializing with doctors' and bankers' kids. He doesn't have the baggage with him that goes along with discrimination and so forth. He just knows to be the best he can be.

Even though that's a good mindset to have, if he inherited your genes, there may be a darkness to his hue. As Blacks mature in this society, at some point he may be judged because of his skin color. Velvet, how does he process this possibility of the inevitable without getting angry at society?

(VB): There are certain income areas inside the box where it's ok to fit in. Even when he comes out of that, you have to be accepted on both sides. Coming from this status to this status, you're still Black. You're just Black rich, or Black poor. That's still saying, we still have to fight.

As well as I did in school and my mother never having to take care of things and having to look the White man in the face, as she always said, "Don't have me coming up there having to look them White people in the face, I send you to school to get an education." She never had to do that, but it didn't mean that I didn't have to fight.

I remember one time in gym class. You can only take so much. We were playing volleyball. You know how you pick your sides. You have a predominately

Velvet and James Brooks

Black side, with three or four Whites, and the other side is all White. When one side is winning, the other side may get a little angry. A girl threw her shoe through the net, and it just so happened to hit me in the face. I can remember saying to myself, ok I can accept this. It was an accident. Then she decided to say what she had to say and that went beyond the boundary. So I had to check that and that was my first fight in school.

From speaking with others, they told me you never backed down.

(VB): I could stand my ground. But they knew, I did not cause problems, I did my school work never missing a day, never tardy, but you could not walk over me. So this is when they find your militancy, so I guess I was about Black power.

Archie, when you played teams like North Side, I understand you all were sometimes called names.

(AS): Yes, we were called names but the thing is as I think about it, some of them meant it. But some called us names to see if they could provoke us by trying to get us out of our game. All they wanted us to do was retaliate. If we fell in and played their mind games, we would've lost. We're not going to be at our best. They did this and I know some of the coaches put them up to this.

But like I said, some were doing it because it was their belief. We had to go out, play our game and do the best we could. We had to overlook the insults and name calling. Like my parents told me, "Someday someone will call you out of your name and you had better be prepared to know how you're going to handle it."

We've always been aware that everything was fair in love and war. But we athletes didn't know that was also true for basketball. Competition was always keen amongst us, but we didn't know they would do *anything* to win the game. The racial overtones during the games, we just didn't expect. We went out to play and compete. But at the same time for many years even before us, Blacks always knew when they got out on the basketball court; it was always seven against five. The seven refers to the five opponents plus the two referees. We found that to be true about most places where we played. The only time we played an all Black team was when we played Crispus Attucks out of Indianapolis. That was probably the best game where both teams were challenged and you saw some basketball at its best.

Velvet, 50 years ago both gentlemen sitting beside you were

1st Row Left to Right: Richard Stevenson, Nate Banks, Archie Smith, Jim Martin & Kim Cress. **2nd Row Left to Right:** Preston Underwood, Bob Bean, Cletus Edmonds, Eugene Wash, Harry Whited, Bob Hopson and George Underwood

involved in a 1963 Sectional basketball game fight with North Side. Did you have a gut instinct that something may explode?
(VB): I did and it was really kind of scary because I had never been in a situation like that.

A situation like what?
(VB): When people are in front of you, you can see them. But when people are hollering at you from the back and all kind of words are flaring...

Like what?
All kinds of words that are not becoming to Blacks. It was ugly.

Did the crowd have as much to do with the fight as the athletes themselves?
I think it was equal in fault. Sometimes the players can control their emotions but when the crowd starts hollering, saying things,

cursing and throwing things from behind you that are going everywhere, tempers start to flare. Now you have innocent people involved in something they should not have been.

As people were hollering jeers at the basketball players, none were meant for the Black spectators were they?
I think it was aimed at every Black that was there, not just the ball players. Once the crowd had gotten angry, things would come out like I don't think they would really mean. But you're saying these things to get a point across and meanness. Now the players are all upset, the crowd is upset and everyone everywhere is all out of context. You're now getting too close in people's faces, now you have pushing and shoving going on and it carried on outside. When you get outside, you think you can get in your car and go home. You're not saying anything and there's people hollering at you; too many tempers were flaring up as feelings were involved. Everyone wants to win in sports, but someone has to lose and they couldn't accept that. It was a bad time in a bad era.

Archie, you were right there in the middle of things. When did you realize you were playing the referees and the crowd too?
(AS): After the fourth or fifth technical. We knew right then that nothing was going right. I walked over and talked to one of the officials because I'm the captain and I'm supposed to be able to talk with these people. I told them they need to get a hold of this situation out here because something is going to happen. They didn't listen and I don't think they cared. And things got out of hand. You could tell it was going to get ugly and you knew it.

The technical fouls were the first domino to fall. What happened next?
(AS): Well, there were a couple hard fouls. When you get a hard foul, that really stirs up the crowd. One of the North Side players was coming in for a lay-up, and one of our guys body blocked him and knocked him down onto the ice. The ref's called a foul, then they called a technical foul. The fans and the players from the other side were upset. We were upset. Finally one of the players came over to me and said, after this game it's over with. They had taken the game from us. After the game, pick a man and hit him. That's how ugly it had gotten.

Rick, I wasn't there at the basketball game. At that time, I was 8 years old. Today, people who are 10 years younger than I am, said they were at the game. The game still lives on. What

was Cletus' involvement in this fight?

(RS): First of all you have to remember that I'm 67 years old now. I can remember generally, but I can say this; I have been told by close friends that Cletus fouled someone kind of hard and North Side took offense to that. But I have to predicate that on it was just time for things to blow-up. It goes back to earlier North Side and Central games and how it was in the locker room before the game. North Side administrators allowed students to have signs up saying "Cletus, you're nothing. Archie, you're a jungle rat. Stevenson, why don't you go sell popcorn for Tarzan." Comments posted like that posted all around the locker room.

We know if students did that, some faculty member allowed it to happen. It was prevalent and at a boiling point with the players as well as with the fans. The fans also knew they had a lot of prejudice activities that they had to live with. The day had come where M.L.K. was on the scene and Blacks were standing up saying it was wrong and enough was enough. I think it was at that point that riots were going on in Los Angeles, things were burning in Detroit and people were saying, "Things have got to change." A change has to occur and if it doesn't, it won't be a good scene and Fort Wayne was just ripe for it.

About two years later, I was working for the War on Poverty and I was going to Washington, DC. As I was just getting on the train, I heard a White lady telling one of the people with her, "This place here is Fort Wayne. It's a real nice place, but they have so many racial problems here." I felt kind of bad about that because they were talking about my home town, but in the perspective that it was the Blacks who were responsible for the problems. They never saw themselves as keeping minorities down and trying to keep them in place, but suggesting that we should feel fortunate for having the opportunity to live in this "so called" great America.

Archie, was there tension building between Cletus and the guy he fouled?

(AS): He and Cletus had been having problems from previous games going back to Harmar School. This had been something that had been ongoing. He had been calling Cletus names and kept messing with him. When you're underneath the basket, we couldn't see what was going on and sometimes the officials couldn't see a player doing and saying things to you. They didn't hear what's being said and if they did, they turned a deaf ear to it. But this guy had been picking with Cletus the whole game and he just had enough. And the way things were going with the game, it wasn't going in our favor because they were taking it from us. We felt like, they're calling all these technicals on us, there's nothing we can do. It's out of our hands now.

Velvet, when the fight broke out, what did you do?

(VB): Well, I didn't get involved in that. As soon as my girlfriend Norma Hides and I got to my car we left. But I could see things being thrown at cars. But I didn't stay. I got out of there. There comes a time when you've had enough. As

The Late 6th District City Councilman
Cletus Edmonds {1945-1999}

Archie said, we couldn't hear everything that was being said on the basketball court. So I'm thinking it was the time to fight back, strike back, say and do what's necessary.

(RS): Your brother, Cletus, was not only an outstanding athlete; he was a *big* outstanding athlete. Back in the day, if you were a tall, big brute, you were expected to be dumb and stupid. But, that was the opposite of your brother. He was very articulate. He was an outstanding student and he could express himself very well.

     Back in that day, White folks did not like Black folks who could speak and defend themselves verbally and Cletus could do that. So there was a built in animosity from Harmar Junior High School until after he went into politics and other things. But that was the whole thing in a nutshell. That's why I'm so glad things have progressed for the better because we have moved in the direction to where we now have a Black President and you can be what you want to be. I didn't say it would be easy, it will be difficult. But you can still set your goals high and be what you want to be and things are much different from back in the 1950s. I'm glad things have improved and we're all a part of the great Summit City. And when each of us can be the best that we can be, it makes our Summit City that much grander things to you. They didn't hear what's being said and if they did, they turned a deaf ear to it. But this guy had been picking with Cletus the whole game and he just had enough. And the way things were going with the game, it wasn't going in our favor because they were taking it from us. We felt like, they're calling all these technical fouls on us, there's nothing we can do. It's out of our hands now.

Velvet, as you look back over the past 50 years, what key lesson have you learned that you can instill in others today?
(VB): If I had to sum up my thoughts in a few words I would say, I know how to act. All of us know how to act. We can act a fool, act right, or act wrong. But we have to learn how to react to all situations.

Archie, the last word is yours.
(AS): I have learned that when people are down on you, calling you names, you can't change that. You just hold your head up, go on and do the best you can. There's always going to be someone who will try to put you down, no matter what you do. I tell kids today, we've come a long way from where we were, but we still have a long way to get to where we're going and you're not going to get there without an education.

Special thanks to Richard Stevenson, Velvet Van Pelt Brooks and Archie Smith
KEKIONGA BLACKS' War on HIS-Story & Slave Mentality

Community Forum on Enslavement Mentality and Historic White Supremacy

Cedrick Tinker, King Mufasa and Prophet Heru

What is Slave Mentality and where does it rank in the hierarchy of Black Community Issues?

King Mufasa (KM): Slave Mentality to me is when you resign yourself to go along with the status quo. For example, I grew up down south. Fort Wayne to me is one of the most prejudiced communities I've ever been in my life. I know there's prejudice here and a lot of other brothers know there's prejudice here, we just don't speak on it. They say, "What can you do man, it's been like that for the longest." We go along to get along. That's Slave Mentality to me. When you don't want to fight and you're content to be kicked like a dog. On the hierarchy of issues affecting the Black Community, I think Slave Mentality ranks the highest. In order to change the other problems, you first have to get rid on the Slave Mentality.

When did you first become aware of Slave Mentality?

Cedrick Tinker (CT): I became acquainted with it through the way Blacks step on each other trying to get to the top. They feel that they have to impress the White man, instead of sticking together.

Prophet Heru (PH): Slave Mentality is one of the base problems with us. I was just talking about it with a friend today – how if we knew ourselves, we would love ourselves. We've been taught to be lazy and to think negatively, so we don't take the time to learn who we really are. We take someone else's opinion and they tell us we're everything but the sons and daughters of God, which is who we are. By us not knowing who we are, it's easy for us to hurt one another.

KEKIONGA BLACKS' War on HIS-Story & Slave Mentality

We're like a young elephant who has been chained to the ground since being an infant. As an adult it has the power to break free, but it won't. People here don't know we're free. So they don't think there's anything wrong with being kicked around, they get their check every month. "I can eat. I can go to the food bank every month." Things are made comfortable enough for us so we won't fight.

(KM): If you want to keep a Black man quiet, give him something he can't normally have. In my opinion, they give us White women. Since so many brothers have White women, they won't deal with Black and White issues.

You give them the daughter you don't care about and they get happy, "I've got me a White woman." They're not going to tell their biracial kids that they're really Black. You're caublasian. (A caublasian, according to the urban dictionary is a person that is mixed with Caucasian, Black and Asian ancestors, a term coined by Tiger Woods) That undermines the Blackness.

When brothers impregnate White women and when they're out of the picture, a White woman can't teach a Black baby to be Black. Therefore, a lot of biracial kids grow up not knowing and are ignorant of their own blackness, so they're not going to address the issue of blackness either. And that's the way it is.

I was talking to a brother a couple of weeks ago and the first thing he said to me was, "I don't mess with those sisters man," and he's just as Black as me. So I asked him, is your mother Black? And I assume you have a Black sister? "Yes but" no, you don't mess with those Black women and you must see your mother and sister as being unattractive? In this instance, the blacker the berry, the juice isn't sweeter to those brothers. This issue can never be addressed by singing and marching. They gave us February Black History Month and the Dr. Martin Luther King Jr. Bridge to shut us up.

Should the Willie Lynch component of Slave Mentality be addressed as a myth?
CT): If it was a myth, it was alive yesterday and is alive today. It started out as a means to control the Black man through the Black woman. It was a way to break us apart and break us down.

Do you really think a White man would be smart enough to devise a plan 400 years ago that would have us confused today?

KEKIONGA BLACKS' War on HIS-Story & Slave Mentality

(KM): Yep. I'll say it again. The White man is a master of deception. That was just small part of a plan that he put together. He's been formulating plans and watching them grow into fruition for years. Did you see *Shaka Zulu*? They tried to trick Shaka with religion. They talked about how Christ was going to get him. But Shaka didn't fall for religion because he thought he was God himself. Since Shaka was concerned with immortality, they eventually tricked him with black hair dye that removed the gray from his hair to convince him that they had given him the fountain of youth. The Europeans said that If they can't win him over through Jesus and religion, they'll "trick him with bullshit." They won him over, eventually leading to his downfall. If White men can come up with simple plans like that, just imagine what they can do.

Is the curse of Enslavement Mentality so deeply embedded within us that it's there permanently?
CT): Whites have a mind control over blacks and they're just sitting back watching us for entertainment.

By Cedrick and Lisa Tinker: Love has no color.
Dedicated to our daughter Laynie C. Tinker, may she rest in heaven.

KEKIONGA BLACKS' War on HIS-Story & Slave Mentality

(PH): It is deeply embedded within us, but with God always comes redemption. Like the Word says, "If we turn away from our perverse ways and seek God with all our heart, then He'll restore us to our land and our birthright." Everyone is going in their own direction. No one is giving God the power and glory. They're giving themselves the power and glory. Until we repent, that's how it's going to be. Once we repent, the curse will be broken. It's a spiritual thing.

It's not for entertainment, it's for survival. Their reason for creating a climate for us to destroy ourselves is to perpetuate their life cycle. They have a fear of being genetically annihilated. If you want evidence that Willie Lynch is alive, many of us have grown up heartless, cold and callused and our kids have grown-up playing Black Ops to desensitize murder. When kids get 19, 20 or 21, its nothing to shoot somebody and the kid walks away before the body drops. That's evidence.

(KM): If you want evidence Willie Lynch is alive, all you've got to do is step outside, look around and watch the news. You've got old against the young, young against the old, male against female, light skinned Blacks against dark skinned Blacks. I was recently at a friend's bachelor party. There was a dark skinned stripper running around discriminating between the light skinned clients and dark skinned clients and she was as Black as tar. "I don't like dark skinned men, I find them unattractive." If you're curious about what other factors help to condition our mentality, how many brothers will pick up a book or watch a documentary? If it's a documentary, brothers don't want to hear that. But if you say here's a DVD with a lot of killing and other BS going on in it, they'll flock to it.

As far as how "Divide and Conquer" works on us, take the example of 3 or 4 Black guys out of work and looking for a job. One guy gets a job. All of a sudden he's happy and won't tell his friends about other possible job openings. All of the sudden his friends are no longer good enough. Some find a good job and move away from the Blacks. Even in the household where the husband and wife both are unemployed. The wife finds a real good job and the husband is still going to Labor Ready. All of the sudden he wakes up and finds out that he is no longer good enough for her. That's why so many sisters have nothing good to say about the Black man.

How do we grow beyond being intentionally psychologically conditioned?

KEKIONGA BLACKS' War on HIS-Story & Slave Mentality

(PH): We have to invest more time in the information we've been given and not take it for face value. We must be more analytical, critical in our thinking, and invest more time in reading and research. We've got to get rid of our mental laziness.

(KM): Some people have to come to the realization that they don't like themselves. You can actually dislike yourself and not even know it. I can remember growing up down south when everyone thought the light skinned guys with the big curly afros would get the girls. I can remember as a kid going to bed praying to wake up light skinned. I would go places with the light skinned kids and stand in the back feeling ashamed, not wanting to be noticed.

I probably would have still been that way until I woke up one day and realized I really didn't like myself. Now I think this bronze is as beautiful as hell. And there are others who only date White women because they don't like being Black. When that light goes off, they'll be like me in trying to promote blackness. There's a man I know who is crazy and went to a psychiatrist and said, "I'm really crazy." Then he'll begin to take steps to heal his mind until each and every individual who hates themselves wakes up and realizes I don't like being black, but I'm stuck here now.

(Cedric Tinker): Blacks are taught while they're young to not like being Black and how to worship Whites and how they look as exemplified by the White Jesus hanging on many of the walls of Black Churches and Black families homes.   White Jesus reinforces Black inferiority and White supremacy.

Are today's Blacks aware of how TV commercials influence acceptance and relationships?

(KM): It's called targeted marketing. Back in the day on the "Joe Cool" Camel commercial targeted teenagers. "If you want to be cool like this camel, smoke Camel cigarettes." Back In my day, Billy Dee Williams had us all thinking we could get ourselves a lot of girls by drinking Colt 45. Now TV has Black women swinging their hair all around in slow motion, long, silky and full of body then there is a Black woman like Erykah Badu walking around nappy headed who is beautiful in my opinion. Advertisers confuse reality. Now you have black women saying, "I want a real man." But you go out there and check how many of them wear their real hair and their real eyelashes. How many of them can you recognize in the morning without their make-up on? Realness goes both ways.

What is White supremacy and why are Blacks reluctant to openly discuss it?

(PH): The answer is in the question. It's because of White supremacy. It encompasses everything from what they project to what we receive. Supremacy means they're better on every level of life and our opinions don't matter. So we comply with the attitude that if I say this or try that, it won't change anything. So I might as well not say or do anything. It's like the ideology and principality out here is a "self-defeating" thought. So we're defeated because we fail to try. Supremacy is a condition where Europeans have a superiority mindset, and we have inferiority mindset. It's a Jedi mind trick when the actuality is the other way around.

Are there differences between Europeans in Georgia and in Fort Wayne?

(KM): They're basically the same. The differences are in Georgia, you knew who your enemy was. Your neighbor next door would let you know he was a proud member of the Ku Klux Klan. He won't mess with you, wants nothing to do with you and he doesn't want you in his yard. That's the kind of White man I'm used to. The kind of White man that I prefer to deal with and the kind of White man I can respect.

In Fort Wayne, White people will hate you, but still hang-out with you. They'll date you, have sex with you. That comes from many of my Black friends who have White women. It's all lovey dovey for a while, but the very first time that white woman gets mad at him, he's going to be called every kind of nigga she can think of and in different languages.

But we don't want to get White supremacy mixed up with White pride. Sometimes it's not that the European doesn't like you, they know too much about you. I don't find fault in a man wanting to preserve his race, because let's be for real, he has to preserve his race in order to survive. In order for the White race to survive, they need to make White babies. He is not like us.

Whatever we mate with, Black, White, Chinese or Mexican, you're going to get a Black baby out of the deal. We're the only race in the world who can destroy an entire race with our penis. If every Black man got himself 4 or 5 white girls and we got them all pregnant, we'll wipe out the White race.

What do you see as the overriding purpose of the White supremacist mindset?

KEKIONGA BLACKS' War on HIS-Story & Slave Mentality

(CT): To keep us down as much as possible and destroy us by sending us off to prison to eventually exterminate us.

(KM): A lot of us are brainwashed, but for White supremacy to be most effective, you've got to believe that White man is supreme over you. And if you look around at the most visible White supremacists, they are some of the most uneducated redneck tobacco chewing backwoods Americans that you could ever meet.

I grew up in the south and spent most of my life in Georgia. Most of the White supremacists I've met couldn't out think me, and my White supremacists teachers tried to tell me I didn't have the mental capacity to go to college. They told me to go to the military or trade school. So I became known by them as that uppity nigga in my classes. They couldn't spank me because I wouldn't let them do that and my mom wouldn't let them do that. I wore nice clothes to school. I could read, write, think, and was opinionated.

One time I got fired from a job in Springfield Ohio. It was a majority of White people and a few Black. The Blacks were happy to have their jobs and they would go along to get along.

King Mufasa and Prophet Heru

KEKIONGA BLACKS' War on HIS-Story & Slave Mentality

The White boys would go around the job cracking nigga jokes and would play grab-ass. One time in a company meeting, being a new guy, I was asked to introduce myself. I said my name was Mufasa, and I want you all to know I been observing all week how you like to play grab-ass, and boot-to-the-ass, and like to tell Black jokes. I don't do any of that. From that day forward, there was a plot to get rid of me. It took them six and a half years to do it.

Why is it important for you to speak out?

(PH): Every great movement starts with a few people or a great person. Once a person steps up and puts everything on the line showing that this is something worth fighting for, it will show the ability to not fear death because we're all going to die anyway. So we might die for something instead dying physically and being mentally broken.

Earlier when you asked me how do you mentally process the idea that when you're enslaved and you want to escape, that you would be killed or whipped, I think we have to detach and de-sensitize ourselves from the reality, or our possible death in order to have hope. You've got to take it with a grain of salt instead of realizing it weighs a ton.

Is the Voting Rights Act still needed, or do the White supremacists from back in the day see the light of fairness and equal opportunity for all?

(KM): I think that anytime you're dealing with White people, you need to have it in writing-on the books. They will constantly change the rules to the game in mid stream. I don't think anything is sacred in a handshake with a White man. If you come back a year later, he will have convenient amnesia. "I don't remember telling you that, boy". With White people you have to pull out paper with signatures and contracts. If Supreme Court Justices say we no longer need the Voting Rights Act, I still think there's a lot of BS going on behind the scenes concerning this issue.

King Mufasa discussing today's Racism

KEKIONGA BLACKS' War on HIS-Story & Slave Mentality

"Black Consciousness Enlightenment at 2013 Frost picnic"

Queen Nefertiti Williams

Any comments about this Frost Illustrated picnic? Queen Nefertiti

(QN): I think it's a great sign of unity in our community, when Blacks come together in Fort Wayne on a joyous occasion such as this picnic.

It is often said that Fort Wayne Blacks are unwilling to publically speak their mind.

(QN): Some Blacks are afraid to speak out because of their mental enslavement, and unwillingness to participate in community activities. I think it's a shame that we have Blacks like that here in Fort Wayne. I feel sorry for them for living in fear. I make it a point to attend everything about Black people because I like to know what's happening.

I interviewed you years ago when Rev. Jesse Jackson was here and you said that Fort Wayne Blacks in general were way behind the rest of the nation. How has your opinion changed over the years?

(QN): My opinion hasn't changed. I think we're still way behind and getting further and further behind. In larger cities, Blacks are working together and becoming more supportive of causes for their Blacks. Here in Fort Wayne we're still divided, stuck in a "me, myself and I" syndrome and not thinking about others.

Do the Churches have a role in this equation?

(QN): The Ministers and Churches need to come together, and I'm looking forward for the day that happens…

But you said that 15 years ago when I interviewed you and nothing has happened yet?

(QN): I said it then and I'm still saying it. Eventually they'll come together, I believe. Something will bring them together. It might be the Lord.

KEKIONGA BLACKS' War on HIS-Story & Slave Mentality

So we have to wait on Jesus, well ok.

Jim, you have been consistently saying that Blacks need to pull together, speak out and express themselves. Over the years have we made any progress in that capacity?

James Redmond

James Redmond (JR):

No! Perhaps very minute. Very few people will speak out and I don't know why that is. Some are afraid of screwing up their jobs and livelihood. Even when you have a job, you should speak out when right is right and wrong is wrong.

And if you don't speak out, things will never change.
(JR): That has been my philosophy over the years and you know that. What's wrong with the other people? I don't know.

How do you cope with the reality that when you do speak out, many will call you controversial?
(JR): When you hear right wing talk radio hosts like Rush Limbaugh and Shaun Hannity say what they want to say with no recourse, why shouldn't I say what I want to say? I speak out because I want to speak out. If I see a wrong, I'm going to speak out about it regardless of the consequences. I don't care about the consequences.

What if Blacks never speak out?
(JR): Things will regress. Just like what the Supreme Court did the other day concerning the Voting Rights Act, we're going backwards. If we don't start to speak up, we'll keep going backwards.

Has Slave Mentality become perpetually on autopilot?
(JR): To a certain extent, it has. We do have the means to turn it around if we want to do that. We first have to educate ourselves to what's going on. The young people don't really know what's going on. It's up to the older people to try to educate them as to what has gone on in this country because they don't know. They only see things the way they are since they've been on the planet. It's been a lot more things achieved for them that they

don't even know about. Like the beatings in Selma, Alabama. They don't know anything about that. They don't know anything about Dr. Martin Luther King. All they know is what they read or what someone told them.

What do you say to Blacks who say they're concerned about issues affecting Black people, but they don't want to talk about past issues like slavery or the Civil Rights Movement?
I feel like this. The Jews still talk about Auswitch. They will never let it die. So why should we let slavery and all of our atrocities die? When Blacks say they don't want to talk about slavery or the 60s, they're shooting themselves in the foot. When they say this, they have not been educated. When my kids came along, I made sure they were educated to all Blackness. Everything that went on before they got here so that today, they are aware. It's up to the parents to educate their kids, otherwise we'll keep going backwards to when we were on the plantation.

Texas has changed the meaning of slavery of the Africans to their being "unpaid interns." How do we keep it real?
Right here in Fort Wayne we have a situation similar to that where Black men don't have jobs, and we have a Mayor in this town who could care less about Black folks and I have no reservations about saying that because it's true. Fort Wayne is going to be just like Texas.

Interview with Ticamarie,
Middle School Student
What have you learned today while being here at the Frost Illustrated picnic?
(T): I've learned that don't hate people; love them and you can learn things from new people.

What made you curious about me?
(T): I saw you talking and videotaping something and it made me curious.

Well I'm just getting people's opinions on different issues affecting our lives. Do you

Ticamarie
(Sorry if I misspelled your name)

KEKIONGA BLACKS' War on HIS-Story & Slave Mentality

like Fort Wayne?
(T): No, It's kind of dangerous. There's too many things going on like killing and people shooting back at cops. People breaking into people's houses and killing them for no reason. There was a baby who got killed in Chicago. She was only 6 months old and she was shot 5 times.

What can we do about that because no one has any answers?
(T): Well, you could get the people who are doing the gang banging together and ask them, why are you are doing this?

How do you remain mentally positive?
(T): I just try to stay safe and pray for the people who are doing bad things

Any comments about Frost Illustrated bringing people together to fellowship at a picnic like this?
Joe Ayers (JA): I think it's about the kids. To bring them out and have a good time and also fellowshipping with the parents. Our community needs to come together to understand that it's the next generation that we need to look out for. Teaching them how to communicate with each other as well as how to mingle with other races. But I think what

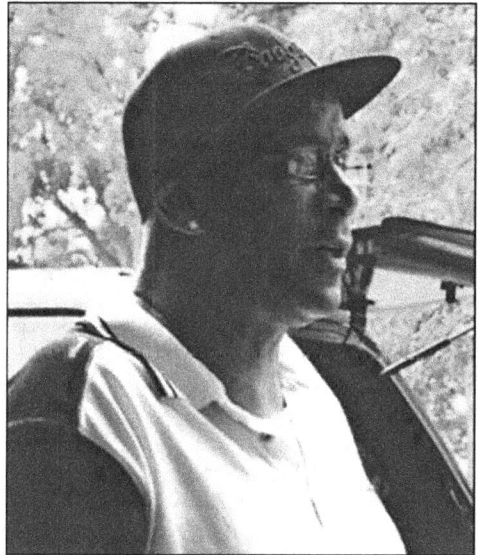

Joseph Ayers

Frost does is bring about communication through the newspaper. If it wasn't for Frost, our community wouldn't be able to communicate within itself about different activities that go on within the African American community as far as successes, education, entertainment and positive stories. I'm really proud to be part of Fort Wayne and have Frost Illustrated as part of my life.

Do Blacks have a fear of expressing themselves publicly on issues?
(JA): Well, I grew up in the Civil Rights Era where churches and resource organizations came out and spoke about issues going on in our society. Now days, people are afraid to speak out because retaliation, and not realizing that by speaking out actually helps the

movement go forward. The generation today is speaking out through music. They're not necessarily trying to make changes within the community. I think people are scared to speak out because they don't think they're being heard.

Do you want to see more Black Pastors speaking on community and national issues?

(JA): My thing about pastors is they're here to save souls and lives. Sometimes it's out of place for them to be speaking out. Back in the day yes, when Martin Luther King, Rev. Dr. Jesse White and Rev. James Bledsoe, were speaking out, that was the era then. In this time and day, they don't speak out as much. They want to stay in their lane. Because if they speak out on the wrong thing concerning God, it may fall back on them. I think in a way it goes both ways. I think they should speak out more but I also think they should stay in their lanes and focus on God's vision to them.

It would take our generation to pull the pastors together and have meetings with them as a group and have them to speak on political and social injustices, including why people are being ostracized because of the color of their skin. Yes, I do feel that pastors need to speak out more, but not necessarily on TV. They need to come to events like this, where they can speak to the public and be hands on with the community. That's what leaders did 50 years ago and you would see them at events like this.

This is 2013 and a lot of people don't respect the Willie Lynch letter. In the letter it says if you keep the slave mindset away from a "substantial original historical base" the mind won't be able to self-correct itself over time, resulting in a generational self-perpetuating enslavement mindset. Are we there?

(JA): I think the time is now to address the issue of slave mentality. As we get older, we recognize the younger people don't have a clue about the slave mindset. They don't understand the bondage they're in as a result of slave mentality thinking. They don't understand it, even tough they read about it and they see it on TV. We lived through it. We lived through racism and they don't concern themselves with racism. It's up to us to teach them about slave mentality so they understand the mindset. Because when we get older, who's going to teach them. If we don't, they may become mentally enslaved and not even know it.

Do you consider yourself a warrior?

(JA): I consider myself an activist of the past, concerned with so-

KEKIONGA BLACKS' War on HIS-Story & Slave Mentality

cial networking. I consider myself a warrior to the extent that I can show people where I've been: you can go there but you don't have to stay there. You've got to know how to get out of the grasp of the storm, because in life, we're all going through something. In the 1960s and 70s, we went through not only Civil Rights, but social and economic hardship. We don't use the term poor anymore, it's now lower income. I just want to show the next generation that you don't have to stay at that mentality. There are too many opportunities out here in life. If you don't take advantage of them, they'll pass you by.

All this starts at home. The parents have to start teaching their young people that they can be anything that they want to be. If you want to become president, go for it. A doctor or lawyer, go for it. Don't let any issue in life stop you, including a divorce, relationship breakup or issues with your kids should stop you from striving for your dream. We've got to teach kids how to dream and go you're their dreams.

Why are events like this Frost Illustrated picnic a good thing for Fort Wayne's Black Community?
Winston Pearson (WP):
This is good for the youth because it gives them someplace where they can go to be with people who look like them. They also see games their parents use to play and they see unity in practice. This is very important and as a matter of fact, I'm enjoying myself now.

A lot of young Blacks have never seen Blacks come together to make any type of substantial change in Fort Wayne. (WP) I don't want to put all Black people in one boat. A lot of young Black people haven't seen it but it doesn't mean it isn't going on. As you can see today, we have Blacks coming together. The more we do this, the more and more people will come out. This is the beginning of what's about to come. Blacks are starting to stand up, we're getting more educated and young people are seeing what the streets are doing and they're not liking it. Don't get me wrong, we have rotten apples, but even with that, there's help with them. Within all nationalities, there are rotten apples who commit to violence and do the things they shouldn't do. But I see hope for us. I see us coming up.

Who is going to promote the need for Blacks to come together?

(WP): I would like to look unto Jesus, the author and finisher of our faith. Number one, our foundation has got to be on the Lord Jesus Christ, of course that's my opinion. Once we put his as our foundation and lean to him, every else will fall into place. Dr. Martin Luther King was big on our Lord and Savior. He just didn't do things on his own. He allowed the Lord to speak to him. It was an anointing behind him. The anointing taught him how to draw people together. A lot of people want to be the big Chief, but there are no Indians. I say that because the lord gives a man a vision and he spreads it. We should all come together. Just because it's not my vision doesn't mean we can't come together and do it.

Pastor Winston Pearson and Family

So therefore, there must be no visioning going on because the Supreme Court has forgotten the meaning of justice, and slave mentality has become perpetual, Jesus isn't here right now and we see no galvanization taking place among Blacks.

(WP): Well, I would like to say this with all due respect. I could care less about the Willie Lynch letter. I rebuke that in the name of Jesus for the simple fact that the Lord says faith is the substance of things hoped for, and the evidence of things not seen. So, even though I can't see it, I know we're going some place. Just because we see a couple fall to guns, the prison system or supreme court justices, God has the final say. I say that we should keep doing what we know is right. Keep pushing and if anything that comes along and comes against us, if we all band together and pray, which is another thing the reverends of the 1960s did, things will work out. The community and the leaders prayed together. And they just didn't march to march, they had Jesus as their base. The love of Christ makes you reach out to your brothers and your sisters.

Is that message strong enough to attract young people?

(WP) It is, but I know it also starts with the elders. A lot of older men and women are scared.

Why?

(WP): Because it's something new. They feel young people don't have any God in them and that young people have no respect. Part of that is the Elder's fought because we have swayed away from our roots our foundation. Mothers are younger now having children. 30 year olds are grandmothers. When I was growing up, my grandmother instilled values in my mother. My mother instilled values in me and now it's like there's no foundation. Everyone's out here freelancing, doing what they want. We need to have faith and keep holding on. Will it be hard? yes! But anything worth anything is worth waiting for. God bless you.

Why is this picnic socially important?
Rick Stevenson, Jr. (RS Jr.):

First of all, I would like to say congratulations. It's an honor to be part of this occasion. It's imperative that we support our local community news papers because this document happens to be our only voice and news outlet that doesn't censor us. It is imperative that we support this newspaper.

Why are Blacks still not vocally and editorially expressing their views?

(RS Jr.): To make a long story short, we have been taught a system of fear and intimidation from the Trans Atlantic Slave Trade and the different mechanisms and psychological methods that were perpetuated on us during our sojourn to America. This has been an ongoing theme from generation to generation where we fear the loss of a job, position or title in order to have things. We sacrifice what is in the best interest of us as a people for us to be really free and have the same equal rights and mandates of other people.

Are the Churches equipped to take the lead of community issues as they did in the 1960s?

(RS Jr.): Whenever you are under a 501 (c3), and you're being funded by the government, there's only so much you can do in an activist role. Different things can be done, but until we come together and unite…

Why do you have faith that things will get better for Blacks?

(RS Jr.): It's like the saying "we walk by faith and not by sight." My faith is that I can see beyond the physical and I see the earning of the people who want to come together. But there's going to take different circumstances that will bring us together. I hate to say that it will probably take more killings and more deaths for us to finally get the message.

We have you and your ministry of talk shows you've been doing for 30 years and bringing me and other people into

Rikki, Richard Stevenson Jr. and Richard III

this forum. But the people have not lamented. They have not danced to our music. So it will take the winds of nature to whip up into shape and hopefully when that happens we'll have a sound structure that we can put into fruition. As old folks use to say, just keep pressing on. That shouldn't alter the agenda that we all want to achieve because I have children now and they're going to have children one day. So I want to make sure they see a better day than we did. It's up to us to instill history in them so they can teach their friends also.

Why is this Picnic important for the community?
Tyrone Cato (TC): First of all, thank you for asking me. I think anytime there's an opportunity for the Black community to get together to celebrate and acknowledge something positive, I think it's a serious statement for the rest of the Black community and it's a serious statement that we need to get together more often on a positive tip to celebrate us being here. The fact that it's a celebration and an acknowledgement of a Black Media is incredibly important because the Black Media has always been vitally important to the Black community. And the fact that we're celebrating Frost Illustrated's 45th year of existence, man that's incredible! This is good for the Black community especially in light of all the rash of violence and the negative things that have been in the media, I think we need to get together more often like this to make a statement. This helps to redefine us.

At any event, too many of us are afraid to speak out and let our views be known?
(TC): We as individuals sometimes overlook the power of a single

voice. A lot of people feel like, hey life happens. There are other priorities and they don't see the importance of speaking out. Sometimes it is out of fear. One of the biggest obstacles to anything you want to do or need to do is fear. A lot of people say it's time, a lot of people say it's money. I think it all equates to a fear of something. A fear of retribution, a fear of ridicule, a fear of criticism or a fear of whatever. But I do think that we as individuals need to step up and speak out and once you do that, you'll see that you are not alone. There is power in numbers and usually you're not the sole voice speaking.

Are we in the mode of perpetual psychological enslavement?
(TC): I'm glad you asked me that. We continue to deal with the aftermath of slavery. It was a serious psychological blow. It was passed down generationally and it's something we're still dealing with. I think it's something that we as a people have yet to over-come.

Some Blacks say that the best way to get rid of slave mental-ity is to stop talking about it.
(TC): Oh no! Once you stop talking about it, once you stop giving it the attention that it's due. Ignoring it is not going to make it go away. That's just like having an illness. If you have an illness, you seek a cure. Ignoring it will not make it go away. We are dealing with a collective mental illness, a collective psychosis. Ignoring it will not make it go away. As a matter of fact, I feel like a lot more attention needs to be drawn toward it. I believe there are a lot of solutions already in existence that we tend to under play and we give the a lot less value than they're due. There are a lot of solu-tions that we need to reinforce and support to deal with the psy-chosis.

Many Blacks confuse confronting their dilemma with not lik-ing White people, so they choose to remain silent to be safe.
(TC): That's part of the trick bag. That is part of the conspir-acy. That's part of the whole intentional conspiracy to suppress us as a people. To confuse us, keep us in the darkness. Anytime you want to say something that's pro-Black, that does not necessarily equate to anti-White. You can be pro something and anti some-thing else. Historically in the aftermath of White supremacy, it's really something that it really doesn't really need to be discussed anymore because we know pretty much collectively how things came about, but as far as dealing with solutions, too many of us get caught up in playing the blame game. It's too late to play the

blame game. You can continue to blame and condemn people for what they did. But I think it has more to do with what we can do as a people than what has been done to us.

Our ability to do something as a people has a direct connection to the dictates of White supremacy.
(TC): Yeah it does, but White supremacy isn't something you can change. I don't think it's something you can eliminate. It's almost like butting your head against the wall. Pretty soon, you're going to end up dead, or unconscious.

I agree with you, but unless you discuss White supremacy to let people know it is a real phenomena that's in place, it gives you a better barometer as to what's going on. Thinking Blacks have to enlighten non-critical thinkers that it does factually exist and that it is not an abstract concept.
(TC): Ok, I agree. From that standpoint you have to be able to identify it in order to deal with it. But once it's been identified, you need to go to the next level and come up with a solution.

I was speaking recently with a Black pastor about slave mentality when he told me that he could not interview with me because I might ask him something controversial. He went on to say that his answer might upset powerful White pastors who have the influence to appoint him to certain prestigious boards that he wants to sit on for reasons associated with prestige.
(TC): We all get to caught up in what White people think. Bottom line is, I really don't care what White people think. I'm more concerned with what my people think and what we think of each other. Because White folks are going to be White folks and I'm not saying that is a disparaging way. People are going to be who they are. A lot of times you can't change that. So you have to find what you can change, what you have control over and take steps from there.

How did you acquire your philosophy of people?
(TC): Just from living and being here. The more that I learn and am exposed to, the more I realize how little I really know. So it's a constant effort to be exposed to things, certain concepts and certain ideals. It's import to study history, because people talk about knowing where you come from. You have to recognize the origins of where you come from, where other people come from and you have to acknowledge and respect that. And you have to put things

in a proper perspective.

How do you speak to Blacks about the plight of our people when they shut their ears to the impact of slavery and the 1960s era?

(TC): A lot of people are uncomfortable with the concept of not knowing. They don't want to look like they don't know things that they should know so they get defensive about it. As a result, they act out in a kind of distraction from the fact that they don't know.

As far as young people are concerned, it's a monumental task. They have so many distractions that we have allowed that have taken away from things that are really important. People talk about obsessions with social media, texting and different thinks like that. All of that is a distraction from important real issues that affect the lives of young people.

The best I can say is, every opportunity you have to affect change in a young person's life, you have to do it. Initially you may think that's insignificant because it's only one person. But change starts with one person and you will never know what you might say to a young person that might change their whole life. It's a monumental task and I think we need to be conscious of the fact that we have the ability to affect change and we need to take every opportunity you have to bring about change. Even if it's just a brief encounter with someone. That's part of the solution.

Eric Hackley interviewing Tyrone Cato

KEKIONGA BLACKS' War on HIS-Story & Slave Mentality

From Chickenbonegate to Religious Pimpology

Interview with Kevin Brown and Edward Young aka Elder Yonah

Brief comment by Kevin Brown before leaving for work.

Kevin Brown (KB): My family moved here in 1956. I've been around. I've seen a lot of things and a lot of changes. In most cases, people think change is good. Change is inevitable.

Everything changes. We have to change our mindset for what it is that we want to accomplish as a community.

Why do many feel we need one key leader? Why isn't more emphasis placed on each individual doing their part instead of sitting back like spectators at a football game?

(KB): No one wants to be the "Lewis & Clark" explorers. And it's because of the barrage of negative attention that would come to them. The White media in this community looks for something negative to dig up on someone who is trying to do something positive to bring about positive change in this community. Just remember, when I was on the School Board, they went back and dug up that I threw a chicken bone at my ex-wife. So it is because of the environment we live in.

KEKIONGA BLACKS' War on HIS-Story & Slave Mentality

So therefore, people have been psychologically conditioned to do nothing and to maintain the status quo out of fear of repercussions.

That's correct.

So Kevin I think we've learned not to eat chicken around you.

(KB): A friend came up to me at work and reminded me of this incident, keeping in mind it happened 15 years ago. It was two White officers who arrested me and on the report one wrote, assault with a "chicken bone." My friend at work came up to me and said, "you won't believe this. I was sitting at home watching TV and there was a guy down in Florida who got arrested for throwing a doughnut at his wife and I thought of you."

(Edward Young): That's the way the media and justice system is.

(KB): If they can't get you, they'll change the laws so that they can get you.

(EY): And that's so unfortunate because they are using everything right now like these killings, the shootings and the bombings to create fear within people. And they always want to find someone who they can pin this stuff on. When you start looking at all the things that are going on in America, they're saying that the guy in Boston who was walking away on the video looks too much like a typical plant. When you watch some of these programs on TV like 24 and stuff like that, the series deals with governments fighting within themselves. One end of government fighting the other end of government. The whole concept is about false flags, about the 24 TV show president "setting-up this", so he can cause that to happen. So that he "can do this" later on down the road to bring "that" about.

I believe, and this is my opinion, that the Boston bombing incident was not set up to hurt anyone, but you had to have that collateral damage in order to make everything look authentic. That's the reason why the other 2 bombs did not go off. They did not want them to go off. The officials wanted those bombs to be found so that they can act like they're tracing it back to a particular individual who they've already setup to take the fall. But there's something else behind that. That's the reason why they couldn't find who they were looking for. How can you find yourself? They have proven time and time again that this is how they work.

When you take a look at some of the things that's going on here in Fort Wayne like the killings, who's actually pushing these kids and killings around here? Where are they getting their guns from? Who is providing all this?

You don't think they're just behaving as misdirected youth?

(EY): I sure don't for the simple reason that, where do you think they getting the guns from? If there is that much gang violence going on in the city, why hasn't anyone done anything about it yet? Why is it always a bunch of Black males who do the small shootings and always the gentile males who are doing the mass killings?

What did you mean when you said the other day that I need to get 50 people together?

(EY): It may take some volunteers, money and things of that nature. Have you ever thought about having a barbecue to kick-off a Think-Tank. To bring together men who are legitimately concerned about the community and who want to legitimately sit-down, talk and discuss it. Not a gay thing, but without females and other distractions.

But females are usually the most vocally bold and enlightened Blacks in this community.

(EY): Then you have a Think-Tank Forum for them.

Over the years I have noticed that a large faction of Blacks are too concerned about how this "activism" may damage their relationship with White people.

(EY): That problem can be easily overcome. You simply ask the person If they're concerned what someone may be thinking about their being involved in a Black Think-Tank? Then tell them to keep their butt at home.

But I've noticed that if you try to persuade or lure a person out of their comfort zone, they will instinctively invent excuses for inaction.

(EY): You tell them that this is about our community and what we need to do to take it back from all the irrationalities that are going on within the Fort Wayne South East Central communities. We need to put things back on a level where, when we want to walk down the street with our wives holding her hand and talking with her at 12:00 midnight, we don't have a problem of somebody doing a drive-by. We may just want to sit out on the front porch and look at the stars or talk with the neighbors.

We shouldn't have to fear anyone shooting at them or anything like that. When you talk to our people, you have to do it the right way and be blunt. "Is he trying to call me chicken?" It's a conditioned mindset you have to deal with. When they have that kind of mindset, they'll show up. "What do you mean if I'm a chicken that I should stay at home?" "What do you mean if I care what White people say about my being here, that I should stay home?" "What is that all about?"

Well if you're worried about "them", stay at home because we're not worried. We're going to say what we're going to say, and we're going to say it how we need to say it, point blank to the point!

What do you say to Blacks who say "we've talked enough. I need a job!"

(EY): Then create one. What do you like doing? Blacks have been ready, but too stupid to understand that and because of our own ignorance, entrepreneurship is not a viable option to them. We're too busy worrying about what someone may say. To hell with that from now on. It's time for us to step up. Our agenda needs to be focused on what we need to do, then do it! Until we consider starting our own businesses, no one else is going to step up and help us.

Why do too many Blacks praise Whites even when it is inappropriate, unnecessary and not asked for by Whites?

(EY): Because they have been taught that this White gentile called Jesus Christ is their master. The name Jesus Christ who is their God, Creator and Savior is the reason why. That's the reason why their heads are so messed up. Earlier you were talking about brainwashing. Brainwashing starts at home by us being sent by our parents to church and Sunday school all the time, to get the wrong information about who, what, when and where. In doing so, Blacks have been brainwashed into believing that this White boy Jesus Christ was their sole master which means that all White people are their sole masters. They've been taught this in school.

Everything they've seen on television that has been good, everything they've read in school books historically is always about White people and their "so called" goodness to the world. Not forgetting the story that they've stolen, killed and raped throughout their history. Not just women, but countries. Same thing they're doing in Africa right now, still raping for her minerals and everything. Now the Chinese are over there for the gas in the ground that the Africans should be able to get themselves, but they have forces blocking them from doing it.

So with all these different things happening, when it comes to our "so called" Black people, this is how we get blocked out and we're not open minded enough to see these things and what's going on. Every four years we vote for a mayor. When are we going to have a Black Mayor. And when we do, what difference will it make. Who will be pulling his strings, telling him who, where and what to do?

You got a person sitting on Fort Wayne City Council right now, for all intents and purposes, isn't doing anything because if he was, he'd be pushing for a lot more to go on over here on the south side. All the things that I see going on around this city, you don't need to worry about who's going to get what. What you should be doing is helping them to get theirs so they can help you get yours. Collaboration is the key. Every other race in this city collaborates together amongst themselves to help each other.

Many Blacks have a 1960s Civil Rights Era mindset and want to do everything through the church. Over the years, that has resulted in a regressive community stagnation. Should pastors still be expected be social, political and economic activist leaders today?

(EY): No, because they've learned the game of **PIMPOLOGY**. A pimp has to keep his ladies in line mentally, emotionally and sexually. The Pastor, in order to control his people, he has to lie to them, control and beat them. How does he do that? By giving them a religion that's not theirs in the first place.

I think most pastors would disagree with you.

(EY): I don't care. If I had a pastor with me right now, I would ask him to show me where in his Bible you're told to form your religion and I will give him $100.00. Show me in the Bible where it told you to form any religion and I'll give him another $100.00, and he can have the $200.00. As a matter of fact, if you can really show me right now, I would give him $300.00 right now! Show me in the Bible where it says to form a religion? There is not one preacher on this earth that can read in his bible and tell that lie. Because they know if they do, they're going to expose the lies they've been telling, because it's not in there and never has been there.

The Bible is against all of man's religions, all of them. It never taught man to be religious. It taught man to worship one individual and that was the creator. It did not teach him to worship John, Peter, Paul, Luke, Matthew, Mark or any of the rest of them. It didn't teach you to worship Jesus. None of that's in there. That is all man's doing. It doesn't teach you to celebrate Christmas, Mother's Day or Father's Day. That's all religious dogma. And because they cannot prove that, I'll sit down with them any day of the week and then after trying to find a way out of that lie, I'll bring question number two.

I'll ask them why do you collect tithes every Sunday and ask for other offerings throughout the week? I'll answer it for you. It's because you're pimping the people. You try to find every little thing that you can misconstrue in the Bible and turn it around to hurt the people so you can control them. They cannot prove me wrong on that! I'll sit and talk with any number them, Imams, Rabbis, Preachers, Priests or the Pope any day of the week.

Are you suggesting they're all agents of White supremacy?

(EY): White supremacy has nothing to do with it really, not along this line of thought. Because the majority of preachers in Fort Wayne who have a 501 (c)3 and are agents of the United States Federal Government and part of FEMA. FEMA has control over them. Anything they are told to do individually or as a group, they have to do it. When they signed that contract to get Federal Grants, they have to follow through on the requirements of getting that money.

That's why I keep telling everybody to read the FEMA directives. For example, if we had 5 bombs explode in Fort Wayne and no one knew what was going on. The first thing that will happen is FEMA will tell the pastors to get with everyone of their parishioners, and we're going to move them out of the city away from danger. We have a camp set-up for them. Make sure you notify the ones who are Hispanic and Black. The rest will be located in a different camp.

Then FEMA will ask, how many of you have guns and do you know anyone in the city who has guns? Then they'll round up the gun owners, because they're next on the list. This is all in the FEMA directives. This is how they're going to work it as disasters, or ever how they need too. Especially if Martial Law is declared.

The NRA enthusiasts around Fort Wayne won't like that.

(EY): The NRA people around here will be against it. That's for sure.

That would create a Civil War in the State of Indiana.

(EY): That will create a Civil War anywhere in the United States. It's coming anyway and is actually taking place right now, only on a smaller scale. That's why all these test beds are going, like the one they just had at the Boston Marathon. Even a Boston news reporter said, "if it was really meant to be like al-Qaida, that massive." It would have been a lot more carnage. It would not have been two or three people dead, it may have been two or thee hundred dead and thousands wounded. The test was done to gauge the responses from the people. So it was just a test.

　　　　Things won't get any better in America until we get away from religion. When we get to the point where we leave religion alone and get back into the scriptures. We need to start doing right by the commandments and laws that are there in the scriptures especially the first 10, and faithfully follow through on them the way we were supposed too. Then we will see an edification of the true meaning of who we are as a people. Why do you think the media is so hard on the so called Black Hebrew Israelites? It's because the media wants everyone to think that they are such a racist group.

Are there any Imams, Rabbis, Preachers, Priests or if the Pope wants to challenge or debate Elder Yonah, contact Eric Hackley. I will have my camera, microphone and ink pen available. Or contact Elder Yonah a.k.a Edward Young on Facebook or YouTube.

Edward Young with wife Ezelyn Omari Ohiero-Young. Wife's former hometown was Cross River, Nigeria

KEKIONGA BLACKS' War on HIS-Story & Slave Mentality

A Personal Perspective of Historic American White Supremacy by Hakim Muhammad

(Hackley) I would like for you to give us some insights into the taboo subject of White Supremacy, a concept that's hardly ever discussed openly in the Fort Wayne Black Community.

Hakim Muhammad (HM): When looking at the system of White Supremacy, I always refer back to a book written by Dr. Frances Cress Welsing, called the Isis Papers. She breaks White supremacy down on a psychological level to where it ties into White genetic survival and their keeping a dominant place in the world.

Dr. Cress Welsing suggests that it exists in all facets of human activity, including economics, education, entertainment, labor, law, politics, religion, sex and war. Actually you can see the residue being played out among darker skinned people. When you have a system of White supremacy, you have a synonymous inferiority complex programmed into the Black mindset.

Historically speaking, it's always light against dark as represented in the Willie Lynch letter. Actually some studies have been done that show light skinned Blacks make more money than dark skinned Blacks even though they have the same level of education. Neely Fuller Jr. who inspired the personal enlightenment of Dr. Cress Welsing said, "If you do not understand white supremacy (racism) - what it is and how it works - everything else you know will only confuse you."

I was recently watching Washington Watch with Roland Martin as he was talking about a study on the high infant mortality among African American women in this country. One would assume that this would be due to socioeconomic factors. A Black woman from the ghetto and being in poverty could perhaps have something to do with it. But they actually did a study across the board where the incomes and education were similar among the studied Black and White women. It was shown that Black women still had a significantly higher infant mortality rate compared to other ethnic groups across the country and across the world.

In terms of how White supremacy confuses or retards our Black Community shows itself through our lack of unity. The Honorable Louis Farrakhan once said, "if you have unity among Blacks, you could basically solve over 95% of our problems overnight."

(EH): America celebrated the 150th anniversary of the Emancipation Proclamation recently and Blacks are fighting many of the same battles from the Jim Crow era and we seem to not realize it.

(HM): The reason for that is the lack of knowledge of self and Black history. When you have a lack of understanding of history, it is said that you're doomed to repeat it and we are. So with knowledge of self, you will break the cycle of Black inferiority. In having a more true understanding of history, we will be guided to make better decisions on a collective level because that's the African way.

(EH): How do we break academic mis-education?

(HM): There's various methods we can use. But for me, I feel that every parent should get more involved in their kid's school P.T.A and other school organizations and advocate for a more Afrocentric educational curriculum. We basically, along with the help of civic and religious organizations, have to become more proactive in the education of our youth and teach them their role in history.

The Honorable Louis Farrakhan gave us an excellent example when he said, if there's a crowd of people and someone takes their picture and you're in that crowd, when you see that picture the first thing you will do is look for yourself. That's the same thing with history. When we start teaching the relevance and importance of history, not with us being a side note but being involved in an important way, that's when we'll see the positive benefits of public school education.

(EH): Your answer may have accuracy, but many Blacks would prefer to have your or most Black people's idea authenticated by a White person.

(HM): Not only is that true locally, it's true national and internationally. Minister Abdul Muhammad, who is a long time teacher in the Chicago Public School System was speaking about this very point in Chicago recently. Whenever he has his lectures, he has a stack of books to illustrate and document his point. In order to be taken seriously by his students, he has to bring a White person to the table. He has to show that some other scholar or White person said it too.

I think this is also part of the residue of historic White supremacy. Basically if it comes down to if I say it or you say it, it doesn't carry that much weight in the minds of many Blacks. But if we show or say that Einstein stated this or the president stated this, that's when it becomes more significant. That's part of the syndrome, "the White man's ice is colder and his water is wetter." The same thing holds true when a Black person is the owner of his own business. Many Blacks will instinctively go to a White owned business before giving a Black entrepreneurship a try even if the Black owned business has been around for decades. The mentality still exist that believes the White person's business is better because of their skin color.

(EH): You've been working for Perry Carpet Cleaning, a business your dad founded, for most of your life. How have you avoided frustration and maintained a positive attitude in a losing battle with White supremacy as it exists in the mindsets of many Fort Wayne Black people?

(HM): I think the key is in having a proper knowledge of self, who I am as an individual in the universe. And a proper understanding of history and of Black people's contribution to every aspect of life. I definitely get frustrated from time to time, but I see my role in the family business. I have to be able to keep things moving and I draw upon the strength of my ancestors who came before me. They struggled, but they still built business and made contributions to a better society. My ancestors didn't let Jim Crow, segregation and KKK White terrorism stop them. So I just draw upon their example figuring, if they can do it, I can do it.

(EH): How does historic enslavement conditioning manifest itself within us today?

(HM): It's more psychological than anything. You can see it in the things we do. Racism seems not to be as overt as it was during slavery when a White person would call you a nigger in public. But the past is still with us, ingrained in our subconscious. You see the manifestation of that in Black on Black violence in the Fort Wayne community with its various shootings. A gentleman was recently killed at the Pontiac Mall.

There's a book that came out a few years ago called "Wild Sanctuary" that documented the various times a Black was lynched throughout United States history. In the pictures that the author presents, you always see a crowd of White folks pointing at the charred remains or the hanging of a Black person.

Then you fast-forward to the 21st Century, you see that same mentality when you look at the reactions of Black people watching Blacks harm one another. For example when a Black says "there's a fight", Blacks will swarm to it and look at the people engaged in watching Black people hurt each other. You can go to various websites and see Black women destroying each other.

It's so sad because when you look around, you see Blacks right there looking at them fight and cheering them on. So what's the difference between what happened in 1930 Marion, Indiana when two or three Black men were hanged in the infamous picture where the White folks were pointing up at them hanging in the tree and in 2013 on the websites where you see Black people pointing at Black people hurting each other?

(EH): What did President Barack Obama's debate performance against Mitt Romney tell you?

(HM): Well again, going back to Minister Abdul Muhammad's lecture in Chicago, which was entitled, "The End of White Supremacy", I think that ties into President Obama's debate performance. White supremacy is not ending anytime soon, but it on its way. He then gave an excellent example by saying if you were on your way to New Your City and you see a sign saying 300 miles, you're not going to pull over and say ok, I'm here. But it's a sign saying you're on your way. You're close. That in a way shows either White supremacy is on its way out or it can still be expressed through the policies of President Obama.

(EH): If a person maintains their same slave mentality even though doors have opened, won't they still behave as a trained dog and not stretch beyond a certain point?

(HM): Carter G. Woodson said something very similar to that when he said, "you do not have to order him to the back door. He will go without being told; and if there is no back door, his very nature will demand one." This is due to our thinking being programmed through White supremacy.

Concerning President Barack Obama, even though I don't agree 100% with everything he's done, I think the symbolism of him being in the White House with a beautiful Black wife and two Black children will for generations shatter the ceiling of our expectations and demonstrate to young people that they can aim for the highest office in the land. The symbolism of that alone is the same symbolism that existed when you go back about 30 years ago to 1984 when Rev. Jesse Jackson was running for the US Presidency. Rev. Jackson's presidential run gave way to President Barack Obama seeing that a Black man can run and compete successfully for the highest office in the land.

Going back through the history of American Blacks, it is important to make note of what we can accomplish based on our individual initiative and successful past performances, that were all achieved in spite of the existence of historic White supremacy.

Interview with Brother Nuri Muhammad, Student Minister of the Honorable Louis Farrakhan

Eric Hackley with Nuri Muhammad

The Willie Lynch Frequency

The "1712 Willie Lynch" letter said that if not corrected within the first 300 years of indoctrination, Slave Mentality will become perpetual by self-refueling itself? My question is, it has now been 301 years. What's the verdict?

Nuri Muhammad (NM): Believe it or not, I had planned to lecture on that today. When Willie Lynch came to America, he was hired by the American White Slave Master as a business consultant. Didn't you know slavery is a business? I said "is", not was. Slavery is a business. How do we know if slavery is not still in effect if

KEKIONGA BLACKS' War on HIS-Story & Slave Mentality

you didn't know what the purpose was in the first place?

Slavery is a business. What's the aim of a business? You start a business for profit. But anyone who starts a business has a goal of turning their business into a turn key operation. What that means is that you don't want to have to be there putting in your own sweat equity at work to be able to get that profit from that business. So anyone who starts a business creates job descriptions, bylaws, rules of conduct, a system that can be put in place where you can be on vacation in Florida and your business is still making a profit even though you're not physically there doing any work.

Slavery is a business and the aim of the slave master is to never have to stand over us with guns, dogs, whips or to keep us shackled in chains. They had to figure out a way to come up with some bylaws, some rules, some system to keep the slaves in check. Thus that's what the public education has been, that's what religion has been and that's what our music has become. That's what tel-lie-vision is, telling a lie through the vision of the programs on television and the radio. It's designed to take the chains off the ankle, off the wrists and put it on to the mind. It's design is to turn slavery into a profitable turn key operation where they don't have to be there with any chains, whips, dogs or guns, but where "we" will keep ourselves in check.

So brother, what Willie Lynch said in 1712 was gentlemen, what I have in my bag is a full proof plan for the control of your slaves. Control right? Now look at what he said. If implemented effectively for one year, the slaves will become self-refueling or self-perpetuating for 300 years, maybe even 1,000 years. The year 1712 + 300years = 2012. Technically, we should be out of the Willie Lynch curse. So why are we still in it?

Willie Lynch said, "I use Fear, Envy and Distrust for control purposes". You see, he's not using physical chains. He's using mental chains. Fear, Envy and Distrust are things that happen inside the head. What's interesting though, my brother, is that the Bible says about man that God did not create man in the spirit of timidity. He created man in the spirit of Power, Love and Self-discipline or sound mind.

So here God created man's brain to be originally on a frequency of Power, Love and Self-discipline. Willie Lynch came to alter the frequency of the original man's mind. So God put 3 things in, Power, Love and Self-discipline, that's the channel we're supposed to be on. Willie Lynch comes and changes the original channel. He replaces Power, Love and Self-discipline with Fear, Envy and Distrust.

Have you ever used a Universal Remote Control? When you buy a Universal Remote Control, they tell you that in order for you to get that remote control to control your television, you have to put in a certain code. Once you put in the code for that device, now you can control that television wirelessly. If you have a remote control car, airplane or helicopter, what makes that one remote control be able to control one car and not the other car. It's because both the remote and the car are on the exact same frequency. When they are on the same frequency, this device can control this car, but this device cannot control that car. So what Willie Lynch did was readjust the frequency of our mind where now we are set up on Fear, Envy and Distrust so we only respond to White people whenever they say move.

So when Marcus Garvey was among us, he was trying to tell us, but we weren't on his frequency. When all of our leaders of the past who are now gone had been telling us things, but we were on a different frequency. But as soon as White people say something, we move to the left or to the right as directed because we are adjusted to the frequency of our slave master instead of the frequency of God. So when God raises up messengers, martyrs, revolutionaries, teachers, we heard the Honorable Elijah Muhammad and we moved a little bit, but we didn't follow him like we should have.

We've got the Minister in our midst right now sending powerful signals to us, but because our brains are still adjusted to that old Willie Lynch frequency, we don't hear him whenever he speaks and we don't respond.

So this is the math real quick. After he says he uses Fear, Envy and Distrust for control purposes, that's for the readjustment of the frequency of our mind when we would be ill equipped to hear the power of God talking to us. Then Willie Lynch said, "I have outlined a number of differences among the slaves and I have made them bigger than what they really are." He said, "I'll put the old against the young and the young against the old. The male against the female and the female against the male. I'll put the dark against light and the light against dark, The short against the tall and the tall against the short, coarse hair versus straight hair, those from different plantation against one another.

KEKIONGA BLACKS' War on HIS-Story & Slave Mentality

So when you do the math, Willie Lynch named 11 different natural differences that we have as people and turned them into unnatural divisions. So he said, "if you institute my plan, it will be self-refueling and self-perpetuating for 300 years, maybe 1,000. Here's what that means. If 11 differences produces 300 years of disunity, that means that every time we accept a new label to define ourselves, we add an additional 27 years three months and 7 days of disunity. If 11 differences produces 300 years of disunity, to get it to 1,000, all we have to do is come up with 36 titles that we call ourselves by.

So now we're not just light and dark and male and female, now I'm a Hebrew Israelite, I'm a Jew. I'm a Sunni Muslim, I'm a Shiite Muslim. I'm a Baptist, I'm a Methodist. I'm a Kappa, I'm an Alpha. I'm a Sigma, I'm a AKA. I'm NAACP, I'm an Urban League Member. I'm a Democrat, I'm a Republican, I'm in the Green Party. You know what I'm saying. We have all these new artificial labels that we have accepted and all it takes is for a people to have 36 differences to produce 1,000 years of perpetual disunity. And you know we have more than 36.

I'm a Cripp, I'm a Blood. I'm a GD, I'm a Vice Lord. I'm a Insane Vice Lord, I'm a Civilized Vice Lord. I'm a Black Keystone. I'm a traveling Vice Lord. I'm a BD. I don't know what the hell is going on. No, you're none of those. You're Black and a Child of God! All the rest of that stuff can go to hell! If we get rid of all that other stuff and we say I'm Black, you're Black, I'm a Child of God and you're a Child of God, well we're are fractions by ourselves but with a common denominator, two fractions can become a whole number. So lets just come together and break this curse once and for all. That's how we do it. I'm not saying that you should not take pride in whatever you call yourself, but it should be subordinate to what God made you.

I appreciate your commentary here today. I wish I had the opportunity to interview you for an hour. I have two gifts for you. A Frost Illustrated and this is our Fort Wayne HIS-Story Reform Calendar for 2013.

Many Black intellectuals won't discuss the Willie Lynch Slave Mentality or its' syndrome because they feel it has no psychological basis. And they think it's a myth.

NURI MUHAMMAD: First of all I want to thank you for the two gifts that you have given me and to tell you on behalf of Minister Farrakhan and our Nation how much we appreciate your effort to continue to unite our people. The Honorable Minister Louis Farrakhan said that our unity will solve 95% of our problems. That would be a lot of our problems gone just from our unity.

For those who want to say that Willie Lynch and his story is a myth, in the Law of the Universe called Karma, in cause and effect, whatever the effect is, there has to be a cause that produced the effect. It's impossible for the effects of everything in that letter to be in existence if the cause of that Willie Lynch was not a real figure. We are faced with the epidemic of those things he said in that letter is based on science.

In terms of finding the origin of things, we can't find the origin of us. It has been said that it is easier to trace back to the exact tree that a 2x4 in your wall came from than it is for us to find out what our original name was before we were kidnapped and brought to America. The ability to trace back our history being that difficult does not mean there was not a Trans Atlantic Slave Trade. It does not mean that we are not kidnapped and made into slaves.

So the fact is that what we see in our people are the effects of this syndrome. This lets us know that he was a live scientist of evil business consultant hired by American Slave Masters to teach them how to use more ingenuity with their business called slavery. They did it then and it's still in effect now. There are some Jewish writers who claim Jesus never existed and has never been on earth, period. But we know because of his work and his word, that he was in existence. So to dismiss Willie Lynch after they dismissed Jesus, it's a small thing for them to do.

HACKLEY: Thank you.

NURI MUHAMMAD:
Thank you, my brother.

KEKIONGA BLACKS' War on HIS-Story & Slave Mentality

Not Too Short For God

My Slave name is Roosevelt Broadnax, but I go by the "Rose." I count it a blessing to be here today. I did not come here to speak. I'm just here as an observer. I was touched by the lady that gave a grand testimony on how All Mighty God delivers.

I was also dazzled by the brother who got up and expressed the effort to end Willie Lynch and all the practitioners of this diabolical scheme against human beings.

KEKIONGA BLACKS' War on HIS-Story & Slave Mentality

I thank All Mighty God for Mr. Hackley. He kind of like nudged me on to come up here. I've been blessed by God in many ways. I want you to know a little bit about my life. I was born in Alabama in a little town called Brent. I was a short person, the second shortest person in the school. I wanted to grow. I had tall uncles, I mean they were real tall.

I asked my mother at a very young age; I said "Momma, what must I do so that I may grow tall like the rest of them?" She said "Rose, in the garden out there we plant our fruits and vegetables so they will rise and grow tall. The only thing I can tell you to do is to get up early every morning and stand in this back door, which faces east, and pray as the sun rises. I had no idea what that meant at that particular time, but I was determined. So, every morning, they would find me praying to God that I would grow. I never even noticed the growth of God until later.

I'm not the best of persons. As a matter of fact, I consider myself foolish. If it wasn't for the grace of God, I wouldn't be here. I've been up and down, up and down, and either up or down. The presence of God's grace has been good to me.

For the brothers and the sisters who wants something to be done about the condition of our people, not only in Fort Wayne, but in the world, must understand that these conditions have been put down by Willie Lynch causing so many of our people to just go in ways that only a God can bring us back from. So I want to say to all of you, if you want to reform, it will be by the grace of God.

Look, I was in jail, smoking cigarettes, and I said that I wanted to quit and they laughed and said "naw, you won't quit." But I said "I will quit." I took the very cigarettes they put out here.....and they had me hooked good. I felt the withdrawal, but I did not put them to the back. I set the pack in front of me and I did not touch another one at the age of 22. Now I am the age 57, by the grace of God. And I haven't touched a cigarette since.

But I took the cigarettes and used them as a wedge to make me strong. See, either I win this battle and beat the cigarettes, or the cigarettes win this battle and defeat me. And I wasn't gonna be defeated....and that's the way to get off of any drug or addiction that you may have. Make it weigh you.....it will bring out the strength in you.

I thank brother Hackley for giving me the opportunity to stand before all of you today. And I thank each and every camera men that stand forth, and I pray that God blesses you all.

KEKIONGA BLACKS' War on HIS-Story & Slave Mentality

Before you step away here, there's one thing you didn't touch on. You were doing repair work in someone's home today. How did you acquire your gift of carpentry? You can do things with ease that others have no ability to do.

Rose: I owned a house when I was married, and the roof was leaking. I was trying to get somebody to fix the roof and they were giving me the run-around....so I said "aaahh," (I was working on automobiles at that time). I thought I wanted auto mechanics for a trade, but I decided to do houses. So I got hooked up with a small company called 'Architectural Builders', and they built houses from the ground up, brand new. I worked with them for several years, building one house after another. Then I left building new houses to rehab with another friend for an another several years. And that's how my knowledge was acquired, primarily through the construction of new homes.

Often times when people go from one career direction to another direction, it gets awfully intimidating because there's so much to learn in obtaining mastery. A lot of people look at the big picture and say "Oh my God, I can never master this." So, how did you acquire the discipline, energy and wherewithal to stay focused to learn what you now know?

Rose: Brother Hackley, it was a natural for me. This is something I wanted to do. I would be talking to young guys and they'd be telling me about jobs and projects that requires a lot of tedious effort, and they would say "no, I ain't getting into that no more," but I'd be eager to go. I like to see something that is not fixed become repaired; I like to see something old be turned into new again. I get that joy out of seeing the transformation.

Did your father do this type of work too?

Rose: No, my father did not do this type of work. I just picked this up because I was looking for something to do. I also did foundry work, factory work, I did all types of jobs just trying to find something I was comfortable with. It's hard work, you know, and sometimes the things that I do is not so pleasing. I've always been a guy with courage. God has given me this courage. I used to do bridges, didn't I tell you that?, and high water tanks; stuff like that. Yes, I used to do sand-blasting on them, paint them, hanging off hoisting chairs.

Over land or over water?

Rose: Over land, water, rivers, train tracks…..yes!

You mentioned that you worked on cars. Is there a fundamental knowledge between automobile mechanics and working on houses?

Rose: There's a fundamental connection between all things that need to be repaired. You'll find this to be true because not only now if I look at something on a house, soon as the brother said something about the camera, this brother said "this camera won't tilt up." First, I was coming on around there…..but then he said "I got it." I was going right over there to see if there was a way to repair it. So, instantly you want to fix something.

How did you abandon the slave mentality and realize the importance of developing you own personal skill set?

Rose: Well, this is what happened to me, I read a book by the Honorable Elijah Muhammad called "Message to the Black Man," and I think that everybody should read this book. This book said that "A time will come in America where the white man would not be able to take care of everybody on welfare and stuff like that." He said that "we should start doing something for ourselves."

Now, there are some brothers that I know, that we all took this seriously; and we began to try to develop ways and techniques to make some money…legally, to survive without having to beg or lay up at the footstool of somebody, asking him for something that we can do for ourselves. What we as a people failed to do, is to do something for ourselves.

We must be resurrected from the dead slave-keeping mentality of Willie Lynch. We must be resurrected! Resurrection is the key to our eternity. Other than that, we will be slaves forever. We must defeat Willie Lynch, we have no other choice. Our children depend on this, so, we have no choice. We got to defeat it, and we're up here fighting it today and we will defeat it!   Thank you very much.

KEKIONGA BLACKS' War on HIS-Story & Slave Mentality

The Spirit of Independence:
A Jamaican Mindset

Interview with Pastor Donovan Coley, CEO Fort Wayne Rescue Mission,
301 W. Superior St., (260) 426-7357, formerly of Kingston, Jamaica

Hackley: Jamaica was colonized first by the Spanish, then the British. How did the Jamaican Natives avoid being the recipient of a double dosage of slave mentality?

KEKIONGA BLACKS' War on HIS-Story & Slave Mentality

Pastor Donovan Coley (DC): Historians tell us Jamaica was discovered by Columbus in 1494. As a result of that, individuals saw us as a great place for Europeans to come to plunder and take our resources. We had the Arrack and Carib Indians. As there was this great fight between the Natives and the Spanish, it got to a point where the rest of the World saw Jamaica and the West Indies as a place where they could also plunder. As the Spaniards economy grew, so did the interest in the Europeans.

By 1655, we had attracted English adventurers such as Sir Francis Drake and Oliver Cromwell. The British literally toppled over the Spaniards. At that particular time the Spaniards had established Spanish Town outside on Kingston and that became the first capital. In fact there are still buildings that represent the Spanish conquest. But In 1655 when the British came, they literally moved the capital from Spanish Town to Kings Town. But instead of calling it Kings Town, they called it Kingston. In 1655, they were also bringing in slaves.

Jamaica has always been a country where the Natives were very resilient. So we have many, many national Heroes. In fact, there was a woman named Nanny who led a revolt. We had an individual named Sam Sharp who also led a revolt against the British. Jamaicans have this incredible spirit of independence for self-determination. Even as you think about Jamaica today, you'll notice they have this fighting spirit and they tend to raise up out of the many nations of the World. Later on we had Marcus Garvey. That spirit of independence has always consumed the Jamaican mindset. Overtime, we have literally decided that we are going to determine our fate as a people.

Europeans are usually smart enough to devise divide and conquer schemes. Why were they not successful with you Jamaicans?

(DC): There is an old saying that says "might is right." There were individuals who thought the power was in the cannons, the gun powder and the guns. Jamaicans not only have the power to fight physically, but also to fight mentally. So they were very good at organizing themselves in tribes. In fact, even today we have a tribe called the Maroons and they actually have their own King. These individuals went ahead and declared their own independence many, many years ago.

So Jamaicans have a way of fighting not only physically but

literally outsmarting the colonizers. One of the first things they did was they created their own language. We came up with a language called Patwa. It was based on English, but then added in other languages like Spanish, Portuguese, French and we came up with our own language to outsmart the Europeans. We could be talking about them and they would not know what we were saying. At the same time, we were also smart enough to speak the English language when we had to. Jamaica had to develop that kind of approach.

Education was one of the key factors causing us not to take second place to the Europeans. The Churches especially the Moravian and the Baptist Church. They sent missionaries to us and there were Jamaicans who literally gleaned, learned and educated themselves to the point that many Jamaicans became missionaries to the other West Indies Islands as well. So I will say, we outsmarted the Europeans at least from a mental perspective and we also used education as a tool.

How was this Movement kept secret?

(DC): Most of the meetings took place late in the evenings. Similar to the American story when you have secret strategy meetings, Jamaicans also were good at doing that. They were also good at having many of their meetings in churches. So the Moravian Church provided a platform, the Baptist church provided a platform and the Jamaicans were so ingenious that they literally were able to gather the key leaders in the community and devise strategies. As they became part of the church, they developed a strategy first and foremost for education. So they started "Basic Schools."

We also had two different types of slaves, the Field Slave and the House Slave. We also had an incredible following for the House Slave. They were for the most part lighter complexioned products of cohabitation between the Slave Owner and the Slaves themselves. We had a group of folks who were emerging as leaders and they literally connected with the Field Slaves. Together they devised strategies so that in the month of October, Jamaica celebrates National Heroes Day. We celebrate a variety of men and women that literally determined the course of Jamaica

Concerning the relationship between the Field and House Slaves, how did Jamaicans avoid Willie Lynch?

(DC): The slave owner did everything possible to keep them separated. However, Jamaicans seem to be a little different. Our mind-set has always been "Out of Many, 1 People." That became our National motto and still is. And I know that we use it here in America as well. We also had key leaders who were dark skinned. Think about Marcus Garvey, Michael Manley, Alexander Busta-mante and Hugh Shearer. When you think of these individuals composed of light complexions and dark complexions, you have leaders and people who represent who you are and tend to give you a sense of "if he can do it, or If she can do it, maybe I can do it."

So Jamaica did not lack in having good leadership in repre-senting all the classes. Hence, we didn't have anything like South African Apartheid or an the Caste System of India. The Jamaican psyche is one of UNITY and we believe the moment you are born of African decent, even though your color may be slightly different, the texture of your hair may be a little different, we see you as one person created in the image of God and out of many, we're still one people.

Why is your History so important for you to know?

(DC): At the moment you go to Basic School, you study a book called "The Making of the West Indies." In kindergarten, you are taught the basics of what happened in Africa. When our people were taken across the Middle Passage, we saw at a very young age the way the slaves were packaged in being transported from Africa to Jamaica and other places in the West Indies as well as the United States of America.

Those images have been riveted in the minds of the young Jamaican student. We start by teaching the truth about what hap-pened in the slave trade. We were also taught that not only were the Europeans the ones we should be concerned with, but the very Africans who sold us out of their sense of greed. We were taught all that at a very young age.

As we move in our understanding past what was taught to us about slavery, we have also been taught to overcome the mind-set that had been taught to us. As a young boy I can think back to when I was going into Middle and High School which was one in the same, that our teachers were even light and dark skinned, and from the Anglican Church they told and taught us that "we were the masters of our fate".

Music was another important thing for us. Do you remem-ber Bob Marley's song Redemption? In it he says emancipate yourself from mental slavery. No one but ourselves can free our minds. We were taught this at a very young age.

I went to an all boy's school. One day we were all gathered around being taught a Latin phrase and that phrase was repeated over and over. My principal Mr. Bruce said, "boys, those words will become the mantra for your life." Here's the translation: "the brave may fall, but never give up."

So at a very young age we were taught that no matter what the situations or what other people or powers might say, because we are of African descent and we have survived everything slavery had to offer, we are going to take lessons from the past, understand who we are in the present, come up with a vision for the future and we're going to call upon the community to support and provide resources we need and we're going forward and make the world a better place. Those were the things I was taught as a young man growing up in Kingston, Jamaica.

Coming to America

On August 20,1982, as a 22 year old man, I came to America to pursue an education. In Jamaica we have many Christian colleges but unfortunately they had not evolved to the level of excellence as some of the secular universities in Jamaica. The school I was attending at the time was unaccredited and was not recognized at the time as a school endorsed by the Ministry of Education.

A missionary from Woodburn, Indiana came to me as I was there in Jamaica at the Christian College and asked, how would I like to study in America? We see potential in you, you have musical abilities and also you do play soccer. And maybe this school in Fort Wayne can use you and at the same time you could gain a solid education. In addition to pursuing an education, I wanted to obtain a marketable degree in Business Administration as well as a degree in Bible and Theology.

The goal was to then head back to Jamaica to influence my country. But as I got involved with my education in America, it dawned on me that I also need a Masters Degree. So after completing my studies at Fort Wayne Bible College, I then went to Trinity Evangelical School in Deerfield, Illinois and completed a Masters Degree in Theology. It was my desire to then head back to Jamaica, but by the time I connected with them, there appeared to be no room for me in Jamaica. But there was an opportunity here in America for me to do church planting. I worked with my denomination here in America and continued to plant churches.

I then left my denomination and connected with other groups and with my wife who is also Jamaican. We continued to plant 7 other churches. Now we have 4 beautiful children and as we look at what we want to do with our lives for the future, we decided to settle in of all places, beautiful Fort Wayne, Indiana. But I'm here to tell you that my long term goal as we move on with our lives is to reinvest in Jamaica.

Presently we're here in Fort Wayne influencing the Kingdom of God. I've taken everything that I am and everything that I've learned to work with people who remind me to a great extent of what we went through as a nation. When you have been displaced as a people and when you've been denied opportunities and at the same time I know a lot of our people make poor choices and decisions that aren't in good judgment. I would like to come along side of and help these people. Here at the Rescue Mission, I am privileged to be the CEO, Senior Pastor and lead an incredible team to work under an incredible board of trustees.

We're making a dent in this great nightmare that many are living. Many people have come to America in pursuit of the American Dream. Unfortunately many are living out a nightmare. Those who are struggling with drug addictions, alcoholism and other issues, they come to the Rescue Mission and we're able to come along side them not just to give them a hand out, but really give them a hand up, empower them and provide resources after they've made good choices. We just come along side and watch them do some serious work. Having them gain stability and strength, we empower them to move forward with their lives so that they can partake in the American Dream.

When you came to America, what misperceptions did you have about the American Dream?

Pastor Donovan Coley (DC): I first want to say that I'm just a student and I don't pretend to speak on behalf of the African Americans community even though I have the skin color. The African American experience is so deep and wide that my heart breaks when ever I reflect upon the struggles and the trials that my brothers and sisters have gone through and what many of them are still going through. So I just wanted to say upfront that I don't feel qualified to speak intelligently on the African American experience.

Coming to America as a 22 year old man in the 1980s, what

I saw in America is that we had a growing middle class at the time. One of the phrases we heard a lot was "trickle-down economics." The idea was, if you encourage the rich through tax cuts, as a result of that, since they're the ones creating jobs and wealth in this country, then the benefits will be passed down to the middle class.

Unfortunately, because of what I saw which was a spirit of entitlement, it would appear as if the middle class and the poor may not have got the message. Even though we want to empower the rich to do what they're doing, if we don't take responsibility for ourselves and if we don't determine our future and if we just wait on the government, if we wait for someone to give us a handout, then that is to our detriment. As you can see, we now have a shrinking middle class.

Unfortunately what I'm seeing when I look at America, I see a place that reminds me of the place I left. There's no middle class in Jamaica. You either have it, or you don't. In America, I seeing a shrinking middle class. There is also a spirit of entitlement and a sense of "we don't want to get up and do the work." I'm not suggesting that the African Americans, Hispanics and other minorities are lazy, but we are still dealing with issues of the past. There is still a mindset that we need to overcome. When we think about the Black on Black crime, unfortunately I see African Americans and other minorities who despise themselves. There is a psycho social dynamic at work right now that I don't fully understand.

Hackley: Let me help you with that one. It's called Historic White Supremacy whose objective is to divide, conquer and brainwash you through emotionally charged confusion combined with distorted African history and your personal sense of good, bad, beauty and ugly. It is through conditions and situations like what you describe illustrates the reality contained in urban folklore (Willie Lynch) that tries to make understandable that which in reality makes no sense, yet is real.

(DC): I agree with you whole heartedly. When I first came to America I did my best to connect with the African American students at Fort Wayne Bible College and it was very obvious that number 1, I did not understand the African American experience and number 2, they did not understand my experience. While it would appear easy for me to interact with the Europeans on campus, there was this division and I started to feel I didn't fit. On the one hand I tried to fit with the majority student body that was White and I tried to connect with my African American peers. I felt as a Jamaican, as a West Indian, I was on the outside.

That was very difficult for me to maneuver. So I did the next best thing. I became part of a church that met on Oxford St., South Park Baptist Church and Pastor Lawrence Howard. I decided I was going to do my own experiment and learn about the African American experience. I'm here to tell you today that I am still learning. But what I'm seeing is evidence of being divided and conquered. I still see that we have great opportunities in America but I see African Americans not wanting to support another African American. It seems to be a division that, if I get mine, I'm going to hold onto that which is mine.

I've noticed how other cultures that come into Fort Wayne, how they come together and pool their resources, support and encourage their own to be successful. I know we have some incredible groups like the African American Health Alliance and I endorse and support what they are doing, but examples like theirs are few and far between. As African Americans, we need to come together even though we are dealing with residue of left over from Africa, slavery and everything that has happened to us, we need to come together and overcome those barriers.

But many of those barriers are a direct result of historic brainwashing and behavioral conditioning designed to keep us confused and divided.

(DC): And I see that happening right now in America. Many of us vote, but we don't know what we're voting about. We vote sometimes because of skin color and popularity and we often no longer vote the issues in line with empowering the grassroots people. In fact, as you think about the founding fathers of America, one of the things they emphasize was education. We have what is called a representative democracy. We are a Republic.

But what we're seeing is that we have certain classes literally taking over the politics of our republic to where we no longer have a representative democracy. We have a small group of people who are leading this nation and they no longer represent us. When you look at the different branches of government, we see there is a 4th branch of government, the self interest of the businesses like the tobacco industry, the alcohol industry and others. What I see is, there is a disparity.

Now you have a Washington that is literally made up of the

elite and supposedly, Washington should be a form of representative democracy. It is my opinion that we no longer have a representative democracy. We're keeping the average person in the streets so in the dark that we no longer know who or what we're voting for. America has also moved away from her moral foundation. As a nation, we need to wake up and see we have been kept in the dark. There is the divide and conquer happening to us in our communities. We have unfortunately Black on Black crime, minorities killing minorities, we're killing ourselves, so we need to wake up!

We saw that happening in Jamaica and realized that while we've experienced injustice as a people, we will never forget it. Every Jamaican child knows their history. However, because of the spirit of self-determination, we're going to do something about it. So education is one of those things. Empowering and employing our people is are the thing we use.

We're going to do everything possible. Tourism is important. Who dominated the Olympics? Jamaica. How smart was Jamaica to go into the Olympics with a bobsled team when we don't have ice or snow? We decided that we're going to do what it takes to get our country on the map. The more foreign investment we can get into our country, the more we're going to be able to employ our people. We do whatever it takes. If it means putting a Usain Bolt or Yohan Blake and all those athletes to represent us, Jamaicans are actually saying "world, see who we are and come support us as we employ our people."

How does knowing your history reinforce your individual desire and ethnic self-confidence?

(DC): Even though I'm sure the historiographers attempted to distort the truths about our history, thank God for the oral tradition and the leaders who kept our stories alive so that we know it in narrative form and it has come down to us. We have different museums all run by Jamaicans.

I think it's important for the leadership of Fort Wayne African Americans to be able to show and tell the story to their people. The Fort Wayne African American Museum ought to be something that represents us as a collective people. I know there are some challenges right now in even maintaining and keeping that going, but I hope as African Americans we can come together and keep a place like that going so that the true history can be shared and be used to shape the minds of African American people.

KEKIONGA BLACKS' War on HIS-Story & Slave Mentality

I really even think the African American church and pastor needs to come back to why we have African American churches in our community. It was not only to bring us together because it was a safe haven, but it was also a place to educate and empower our people in areas of theology that is bionically based, but even in sociology to let our people know who they are as far as being created in the image of God. I believe there are other African Americans from other religious faiths, not only the Christian faith but the Muslim faith. Whatever faiths we have in the community are there to help shape our culture. We need to call upon them to educate our people from the smallest to the oldest.

You recently attended a national summit with other Rescue Mission executives. What did you learn that you didn't already know?

DC): The Fort Wayne Rescue Mission is part of the Association of Gospel Rescue Missions made of about 280 Rescue Missions through out our nation and I happen to be on the board of trustees. Here's one thing I've learned Eric, when I went there I realized that Rescue Missions, just like other parts of our community, are going through changes. We're having a diverse group of people come to us for our service. Rescue Missions are making adjustments to be inclusive. Some Rescue Missions have been places where people have been discriminated against. What I learned is that Rescue Missions exist to provide through the power of Jesus Christ, a home for the homeless, food for the hungry and hope for the future.

But we should also empower, regardless of what their background or what sexual orientation is, or what it is that they're struggling with, we ought to be places where anyone can come. Then we should love them, empower them and urge them to become better citizens in their community. So what I learned in Houston, Texas was that at Fort Wayne Rescue Mission, we need to be more inclusive and we need to be more supportive of what's happening in our community. We also need to address the real issues and concerns that people are struggling with and not just preach to them, but to empower them.

{1813~2013} Bicentennial Salute to Shawnee Chief Tecumseh

Jada Baymon

KEKIONGA BLACKS' War on HIS-Story & Slave Mentality

Interview with
Michelle & Jada Baymon

I recently met two beautiful young women walking through a local department store. What caught my attention about these ladies was the aura that had encased their presence as they navigated their way through the customers walking about freely. It seemed as though everyone just stepped aside as this mother and daughter combination was headed in my direction. They both were larger than life and had a presence as large as a highway billboard, even though they were standing at 5'4" and 5'2" inches.

Chicago Bears and Shawnee Football fans Michelle and daughter Jada Baymon

KEKIONGA BLACKS' War on HIS-Story & Slave Mentality

Mom was wearing a #23 Chicago Bears jersey and daughter Jada was wearing jersey #34 of her Shawnee Middle School Football uniform. Walter Payton was her favorite football player.

Wow! Needless to say I stopped them. We talked and we set a date to meet at the Pontiac Branch Library for an interview. I had never experienced anything like this before. As I was speaking with mother and daughter, Mom's eyes were so focused into my eyes as I was speaking with her daughter, I had no doubt that she could see the inner workings of my brain.

As we were parting company, we shook hands. I was being gentlemanly when I grabbed her hand and she dropped me to one knee with her vice grip hand clasp, warm smile and sincerity.

Hackley: How did you become interested in playing football?

Jada: At the beginning of my 7th grade year during student registration for school, the coach happened to be standing near-by and I said, "Mom, I'm going to try out for football." She got excited, but I really didn't want to do it. But I still signed up and after a few practices, I started to like it.

Hackley: Mom, when you saw that your daughter had made this decision, how did you feel about it?

Mom: I loved her decision and I love football. I also had a son Jarvis who is 10 years older than Jada, who played for 7 years in the Metro Football League in Chicago.

Jarvis Jackson

KEKIONGA BLACKS' War on HIS-Story & Slave Mentality

Hackley: What was your position?
Jada: Linebacker

Hackley: What did you do on end sweeps when you had many blockers and the ball carrier running right at you?
Jada: I just focused my attention and went for the tackle. That's all you can do.

Hackley: How did the guys feel about you being on the football team?
Jada: They talked about me for weeks until I showed them that I wasn't playing, that I was serious. I knocked a boy out cold! He was down and out!

Hackley: Were you the only young lady on the team?
Jada: No. There were 2 last year and one this year.

Hackley: How did your girl friends feel about this decision?
Jada: They were excited.

Hackley: Why didn't they want to be on the team?
Jada: Because they weren't tough like me. They're not as daring as I am. I am strong, but I don't fight. I do what I have to do. By me playing football shows the guys that girls can play too.

Hackley: How did you instill this inner toughness in your daughter?
Mom: I wanted her to stand and let them see that she was not weak. That she was going to be a part of this team and for the guys to accept the fact that a girl will be on the team.

Hackley: How did the men in your family feel about your decision?
Jada: My uncles and my brother loved it. My aunts didn't really care for the idea.

Hackley: What was your scariest showdown?
Jada: In one game, a guy got the ball and ran straight at me.. I wasn't ready for that and he knocked me on my back. The second time, I tackled him.

Hackley: Do you plan to play high school Football?
Jada: Yes I do, either at Bishop Luers or Northrop.

Hackley: What do you want Jada to learn from he school experiences?

Mom: With her being in Middle School, I wanted her to take on the challenge. I'm not sure about her playing in high school because that's another level. The first thing we have to remember is, she is a young lady and the athletes are not as gentile as they are in middle school.

Hackley: How has sports helped her maturity?
Mom: In taking on more challenges, not being afraid or wanting to quit and in giving her best. In standing up for what you believe and following through on your commitments. As far as her schooling is concerned, these attributes will help her achieve academic goals and in qualifying for scholarships. Being able to stand, be independent and self-reliant is what I want her to be.

Hackley: What are your favorite classes?
Jada: Band and Math. The instrument I play is the tuba. I like it because it's big, loud and it stands out. I choose the tuba because it's beautiful and I could be different. And also because no one else picked it.

Hackley: After high school and college, what do you see for yourself?
Jada: I see myself as being a professional singer or lawyer. I sing in my choir at church. As far as being a lawyer, I love to argue.

Hackley: If you had the opportunity to speak to young ladies on their way to middle school, what advice would you have them about the importance of stepping outside their comfort zone?
Jada: I would tell them to it's tough, but keep your head up high. And don't let anyone discourage you.

Michelle with daughter Jada Baymon

KEKIONGA BLACKS' War on HIS-Story & Slave Mentality

Mrs. Stith wanted to be an attorney, not a teacher.

HACKLEY: You're looking so calm and poised, but I know you, your daughter and granddaughter have been involved in a war over at the African American Museum for the past many months. As of April 24th, 2013, what was the status? Has everything been resolved?

No! It has not been resolved, and I don't think it will really ever be resolved. It has not been the past few months that I've had problems with the Museum board, it has been approximately two years that I've had issues and disagreements with the board. It is not settled and I don't think it will ever be settled. Things at present are in limbo.

Will the Museum survive?

On February 18, 2013, I was locked out of the Museum. I was interviewed by the newspaper and TV stations, the very first thing I said to them was, this is perhaps the end of what we know as the

African American Museum. I still feel that day was the end of what we know as the African American Museum. I wish, but I have great doubts that it will continue.

What originally gave you the idea to start an African American Museum?

In 1975 when Fort Wayne began to celebrate America's bicentennial, there were no Blacks involved in the actual planning of the 1976 celebration, America's 200th anniversary. Gail Grier who was CEO of the Urban League at that time, contacted me and Miles Edwards because we were both educators and natives of Fort Wayne. She asked us if we were interested in working with the committee to help provide activities for African American people in this celebration. That is how I became interested in Fort Wayne Black History.

I was born here and there have been Blacks here ever since I can remember. I went to the library and they had very little information on African American people. They had a folder that had a few clippings like, Marjorie Wickliffe had written a history of Fort Wayne with no dates and it was mostly about her family. The other clippings were incidental, of no major importance concerning history. Then I went to the History Center, which was the Fort Wayne Museum at that time, and they had four pictures of Black people. I was so elated when I saw those four pictures. They had been taken in 1936 and I knew a lot of people on those pictures. That increased my interest in the Black History of Fort Wayne. Those pictures had been taken by the Red Feather Agency at the Wheatley Center which was a recreational center for Blacks in the 1920s.

I became interested in documenting our history up to this time. It hadn't really been done. I started out interviewing 6 elderly people and I turned those tapes over to the Allen County Museum. I took pictures and for the first time ever, we were able to have an exhibit of Black People at the Allen County Museum. When I interviewed those six people, the thing that was most difficult was in remembering dates. People could tell you what happened, but they found it difficult to accurately come up with the dates of when it happened. But it was very interesting to research, put dates on places and names on people. I began working on this project in 1975 and I'm still working on it presently, almost 40 years. This was the beginning of my interest in being involved in Black History in Fort Wayne.

KEKIONGA BLACKS' War on HIS-Story & Slave Mentality

You mentioned 1976, didn't you and your husband Harold have the 1st Juneteenth Parade that year?
Yes we did. We had the largest celebration that has ever been held in Fort Wayne. I imagine about 10,000 people attended. We had the celebration in Memorial Park and it lasted all day. We had a parade and I had asked Mayor Richard Hatcher of Gary, Indiana to lead it but at the last moment he was not able to honor the engagement. Fort Wayne Mayor Robert Armstrong led our Parade. We paraded from the Lincoln Life parking lot on Calhoun St. to Memorial Park. I have pictures of it and it. The parade was fabulous. It was the largest Black Parade ever.

I have been collecting and savings things about Black people all of these years. I stored them in my husband's warehouses and my basement. I had many things which enabled me to do traveling exhibits like in Headwaters Park, Old Fort YMCA, and the City-County building. All this was actually the beginning of the birth of the 1st African American Museum in Fort Wayne.

There was a lady named Ann Fairchild who worked for the History Center in the 1990s. She was over the education department. Ann thought there should be more involvement of African American people at the Museum. We were involved with the downtown Museum for many, many years. We worked out of the Museum and did projects that were sponsored out of the Museum.

Ann thought there should be an African American Society and it was through her initiative that we called Blacks together and organized and formed what was known as the African/African Historical American Society Museum. The reason it is called African/African is because there are Africans who are Africans, not mixed with anything. They're pure African. We have slash African Americans and we're mixed with everything. That's why we have the title, African/African American Historical Society. Out of the birth of the society, eventually it was decided that we needed a museum. Will Clark and Ann Fairchild were very instrumental in helping in the organization of this project. Also there was Mary Ray and Miles Edwards who were educators, Carol Cartwright and a few others along with myself are the founders of the African African American Historical Society. The Museum came into being on February 1, 2000.

In the beginning, this was something new. It caught the eye and attention of the people who were interested in it. We had fundraisers and gatherings and big dinners. People donated food, We began by informing people of what our intentions were. We had quite a following at that time. What made it so interesting was that our following was not all African American people. We had a sizeable amount of other people and through the early stages, our effort was highly integrated. There was enough interest and we felt that we could make it a successful museum. We told people this was necessary because we do have a History Center. But there is not enough room. They would give us a small space for an exhibit. But we were limited and had to get approval for space and what kind of exhibit we could present. Being that everything was so limited, we decided that we needed our own museum and the interest was there.

What was the Black Church involvement in this initiative?
None. The Church was not instrumental and they did not have great involvement. As far as community issues are concerned there is interest and cooperation among the churches. But in other areas, there is no cooperation among the Black Churches. They had little involvement in the beginning of the Museum. Turner Chapel is where we were allowed to have our first gathering and dinners, free of charge. I am a member of that church.

I had an exhibit on the African American Churches of Fort Wayne. We took a survey in the year 2000 of the 105 Black Churches. I was the photographer. I had taken pictures of all the churches and had a little bit of history on each of them. Some of the Ministers sent me their histories. The churches did not cooperate when I had this huge exhibit of African American Churches, but I did have them all in our main exhibit. The Churches and Museum would have both greatly benefited by greater involvement from the churches.

I was born in Fort Wayne in 1928. There were very few Black people here. During my early childhood years, there were under 1000 Black people in Fort Wayne. In 1918 a lot Blacks were recruited to come to Fort Wayne to work for the Pennsylvania Railroad. Bass Foundry sent representatives south to recruit Blacks to come and work. International Harvester brought Blacks to Fort Wayne from Ohio to do janitorial work. It was not until the 1940s that Blacks were allowed to work on machines at Harvester. The beginning Blacks worked for 26 cents per hour.

It was in the 1940s that Blacks came to Fort Wayne in mass. President FDR passed a Fair Employment Law on June 25,

1941. World War II was beginning and factories were beginning to open and FDR said, "any factories making ammunition and products for the government, had to hire Black people. Because of that, the population of Blacks in Fort Wayne more than doubled. In the 1940s, we had 2500 Blacks. Most of the people came from Alabama. From the 1940s to 1960, we had over 5000. In the 1990s, the population of Blacks doubled again to over 14,000 and I've traced the roots, they're mostly from Alabama.

In the 1930s when you were in elementary school, did teachers care about you becoming educated?
My circumstances were a little bit different than many of the other black children. Speaking specifically of the experiences I had, I went to Justin Study School in Westfield and today I still have my records from kindergarten through the 6th grade. I did real well at Study School. The teachers were very nice to me. I found that there were certain teachers who were nice to black children and there were other teachers who wrote them off saying, "those children will never succeed." I can say that it depended on the child and I cannot say I was discriminated against in elementary school. As a matter of fact, I became the teacher's pet. I represented our school in the 3rd grade when 10 students traveled with Sgt. Dunnivan, the Humane Officer when they had "Be kind to animals week" and kids traveled to different schools to speak. I also represented Study School in a spelling contest that was on WOWO radio. I had been the type of child who had been motivated and encouraged to do my best in school where a lot of kids did not receive the attention and motivation from family.

Washington Middle School was mediocre. When I first went there from Study, there were only 5 kids. Most Blacks were sent to Jefferson because they said that was the dumb school. As far as Central High School was concerned, we were never motivated. The Dean never called you in to tell you what courses to take. They took it for granted that all black kids were not going to college. So you took a general course or vocational classes. They did not pay and special attention to Blacks as far as I know. We were not allowed to attend the school dances. When Central won the Indiana State Basketball Tournament in 1943, Blacks were turned away from the dance celebration, but the Blacks on the team could attend. Although I worked on the HS newspaper, we could not be cheerleaders. There were things that we were denied. I achieved and did well because I had relatives who were interested in my doing well and pushed me.

As far as the education of Blacks in Fort Wayne is concerned, we didn't have any Black teachers. The first Black teacher
in history of Fort Wayne was Gloria Morton Finney. She was hired
in 1952 and taught at Hanna School. I think she was hired under
Aaron T. Lindley who became Superintendent also in 1952. In
1954, two more Black teachers were hired. Mary Ray was the
second hired as a 4th grade teacher at Hanna School. Pauline
Ford was the third Black hired and she taught at Hamar School. It
was very difficult for Blacks to be hired in education in Fort Wayne.
That is why we have so very few now.

We had a very late start when Fort Wayne realized they
needed Black teachers. In 1970, teams were hired to go to southern colleges to recruit Black teachers and I was hired for that purpose. My recruiting territory was North Carolina. However, the
most teachers were recruited and brought to Fort Wayne from
Stillman College in Tuscaloosa, Alabama. They were recruited by
Andrew Dodson. We also had Ernest Lavender and Georgia was
his recruiting territory. That is how we got the first large Black
group of teachers in Fort Wayne. That was the brainchild of Ms.
Oberland who was in charge of employment at that time. We have
never had an abundance of Black teachers in Fort Wayne Community Schools. Today we're fortunate to have a Black Superintendent, but we are lacking Black teachers in the Fort Wayne
Community School System.

We are lacking because the pay was not good. Blacks
working in the factories made more money than teachers. The
first year I started teaching, my salary for the year was $3,600.00
and I still have that contract. People working in other areas made
much more money. The pay has not been good and I think that is
the reason we haven't had many teacher colleges in the north.
Most have been in the south. Ball State has a teacher's program,
most northern schools do not.

Why did you become a teacher?
I never wanted to be a teacher. I wanted to be an attorney. The
reason I became a teacher was, I had been out of college for
some time. I had attended Wilberforce University, and Wilberforce
lost its accreditation while I was there. I dropped out of college.
The next year I went to New York to study drama at the Negro
American Theatre and I met my husband Harold and got married.
We came back to Fort Wayne and I had a child. I had started

working at General Electric and my husband said "I want you to go back to school." So I went to St. Francis at the age of 27.

Was Harold Stith still knocking people out at that time?

My husband had been a professional fighter but he had an injury to his thumb and could no longer fight and that's why we left New York and came to Fort Wayne. We came here for a vacation, he loved Fort Wayne. Harold thought this was the land of milk and honey. He decided he was going to stay and he got a job at General Electric.

Did you ever personally see him fight?

Oh yes, yes, yes. I saw him fight at the Madison Square Garden. He was quite outstanding. He was 4th contender for the World Lightweight Championship. In those days, they didn't make the money they do today. And Blacks guys had a very, very hard time. All their managers were White and sometimes they had to take a fall or throw a fight to get a fight. I know all about the dirty politics of boxing. Harold was outstanding, but he never reached his full potential.

Were you nervous sitting in the stands watching him fight?

I felt great sitting among the audience. He had to fight mostly white guys and I'd be rooting for him when everyone was looking at the me like I was crazy. Sitting among "them" and rooting for him, I felt great, like I was a special person. No one knew my connection to him, but is was very special connection because we were married.

Back in the classroom, did you have any misconceptions about teaching Black kids?

Yes I did. I was the first Black teacher hired at McCulloch School. Because I was the first Black teacher hired at McCulloch School, they thought because I was Black, I had answers to all the Black kid's discipline problems. They gave me all the problem Black kids from the 2nd and 3rd grades. I was hired to teach 2nd, but they decided to give me a split grade. I got in that classroom and I could not believe the behaviors that I was experiencing. So as a band new teacher, I went to the principal and I told her I had been hired to teach 2nd grade. Not only was I given a split grade, I was given difficult children. I told her I was not going to teach. I will leave the school and find another job. I refused to teach. They were appalled that a brand new teacher had the nerve to approach my authority and tell them exactly what she felt. I ended up with a regular 2nd grade class and a horrible first year.

I still had a lot of discipline problems. In being a new teacher, it was really rough and I said if I can make it through this first year, I'm through with education. I'm getting out of the class-room. I don't want to be a teacher. But I made through the first year which was the roughest year I've ever had in my life. Many of those kids grew up to be troublesome adults and I have tracked a few of them. Even now, they still have problems. Later on that same year, they did hired another Black teacher, Mary Alice Turner to teach kindergarten. We were the first Blacks and we had some very difficult days. I did not enjoy my first year at all.

How were you able to understand the essence of your Black children's problems?

I think that "walk a mile in my shoes." Many of the teachers had never walked a mile in those kid's shoes. They did not understand the home life experience of these kids and the environment in which they lived. They children had problems that were unique to them. Some teachers never experienced those problems or how to reason and work with them. How to know how the children were being neglected. I was doing the lunch count one morning and a little Black child came in. He said to me, "I want to talk to you!" I can't talk to you now, I'm doing my lunch count. He tapped me on my shoulder and said, "did you hear me? I said that I want to talk to you right now!

The average teacher would have gone off. I set everything aside and told the children to lay their heads down on their desks and I walked outside the classroom with the young man. I asked him, what was wrong? He told me his father had given him a terri-ble beating this morning before he came to school. I asked why? He said, "because I couldn't find my shoes." He said, "I hate my father, he always does that to me." Even now it hurts me to talk about this incident. He said, I hate him and I would like to pick up a gun and kill him." He was a special kid with special problems and I had to work with him because I knew the circumstances he had to face.

Another time we had a Red Cross Fund Drive and someone in the class stole all the Red Cross money. I addressed the class asked that whoever stole the money, to write a note and let me know who did it and I promised they would not be punished. I just wanted to know why? The girl who stole the money wrote a note and said her sisters and brother were hungry so she stole the money to buy donuts for breakfast. Things like that make you aware of the circumstances and the kind of children you're working with and they really needed you.

Some of my children had low intelligence scores. For example Fs and Ds. I said oh no! They should have a better intelligence rating that an "F" or "D." That gets passed along with the kid. There is a special test, a culture free test for Black children it's called a Culture free test. I looked into all those kind of things and I insisted that children have culture fair tests to bring their intelligence scores up. They did not know how to take tests. Sometimes as soon as I gave the instructions, some would be finished with their tests. As I am explaining, they are filling in answers. Not reading the questions, but marking answers. There were things I knew and had experienced myself that could help these children. That's why I spent all my years teaching in the inner city. I had transferred to Lindley Elementary when it first opened and when my transfer came through. I said no my children need me here at McCulloch. I stayed there until it closed.

Does this have anything to do with why you became an advocate for Black people ?
Yes because I knew there was a need for someone to do that. Many were qualified, but few would step up to the plate. I have always been active and part of the community. I grew up in Westfield and we had a tight relationship out there. I know the hardships. I grew with kids from a family who were so poor, they didn't have a change of clothes. My mom would feed people, even though we were poor too. But there was always some poorer than you. There was no snobbishness at all. I knew a boy who was so poor he had to wear his sister's clothes.

I grew up in this community and my heart has always been with my people. I always felt someone needed me and I felt good about it. I was just looking at something that I had done the other day that I could not afford, but there was someone in need, so I bought it. I have been feeling so good ever since I did it. I've always had a heart for the underdog. I've been the underdog myself, but there's always someone worse off than you. And I have always been a person who was willing to speak what I thought.

What made you fearlessness in being verbally assertive?
What gave me the ability to be assertive? My mom trusted me when I was very young. She would tell me, "you go to your cousin

and tell them I need to borrow a cup of sugar." Mom could depend on me to go and return with a cup of sugar. What ever the message, she didn't have to write a note. She could tell it to me and I'd go. I was friendly and would play with all the kids in the neighborhood, no matter if they were barefooted and raggedy, I would play with them. I had a girlfriend who was deaf and dumb and she would stop by my house about every morning and have oatmeal with me in the summer. I've always been a part of the crowd. Not isolating myself or wanting to be alone or be selfish. Even now I might call my brother and ask, what are you guys doing for supper? Then I'd say, don't cook. I'll bring supper. Just wanting to share has been my whole life.

Do you envision Blacks being a major player in this society?
No, I don't see it because some let the past keep them down and I figure you have to rise above and forgive those who have harmed you. When an opportunity arises, you have to take advantage of that opportunity. For example, a lot of us do not vote. It is very important for us to vote now that we have the right to vote. You cant say that my one little vote doesn't count. If you are interested in who is going to make the laws that you're going to have to live by, the only way you can be represented is to vote.

In the constitution for example, the 13th, 14th and the 15th are the key amendment that benefitted us. We were not considered as whole human beings. We were considered as three fifths of a person and as property. The 13th amendment freed Blacks. The 14th amendment made Blacks US citizens and the 15th amendment gave all men the right to vote. I'm just saying that the laws that "held us back" then are over with. The laws that said you cannot testify in court because you're Black, the law that said you can't live a certain place because you're Black or the law that said you cannot do certain things because you're Black, the law allowed for slavery to exist. In fact, in 1831 there was law that was passed that you could not attend school, even in Fort Wayne. In the State of Indiana, Blacks were prohibited from doing a lot of things. You cannot dwell on those negatives. As Black people, we've got to work extra hard to rise above the circumstances.

I recently read an article in the paper which concerned me. The PNC Bank on Calhoun St. has been recruiting Burmese people working there. They currently have 5 working there now. They have two in top management and three as clerks. They have not recruited Blacks to work in that bank. You don't see one Black person working in that bank where they have a larger Black clientele. I'm just saying that there are still things that are against us as a race of Black people. We need to stick together, rise up and fight those things to make sure we get a piece of the pie.

I feel Black people need a new birth. They need to realize that they're not going to be recognized as full first class citizens unless they demand it and take advantage of all the opportunities available. But we're doing so many things to degrade ourselves like wearing your pants down with your underwear showing, hair standing up wildly all over your head, shooting each other and things that you say, are not cool. Our music is not good for our children. There are so many things that our race must fix for ourselves.

How do "scared" Blacks end the fear of being able to look squarely into the eyes and speak directly to White people?
I think that depends on the person. We need to read and be more knowledgeable. We need to be aware of the things that harm us. We need to be aware of the things that are good for us and we need to participate more in the community. For example, if you wanted to talk to me about what recently happened in Boston, I want to be aware of the incident that happened that I can communicate with you on the same level if you want to communicate with me and I've only been listening to crazy stuff and not read newspapers or watch the TV news. I'm not educating myself to current events.

I have to be well aware of the issues. I have to know what I'm talking about so I can communicate with you. I can look you in the face and communicate with you and not be afraid. I think some may feel inferior to a person because you're not up on what ever that subject is. Sometimes a Black person may drop their head when talking to while person because of the education background.

If your educational background, If your daily background, If you live the kind of life where you're knowledgeable, then you won't be afraid to look a person in the eyes and communicate with them on the same level. I'm not afraid to communicate with people. If you're talking about the astronauts and high tech subjects, I'll ask you to inform me about that because I'm not up on it. But I think generally speaking, it's going to take you being aware of the things that are happening around you and the things that you need to know to be a productive citizen.

KEKIONGA BLACKS' War on HIS-Story & Slave Mentality

Scott Williams please tell us about your dad Jesse Williams, the founder of Jesse and Sons Barber Shop and how you got into the family business.

Scott Williams with customer Reynald Amazan

Of course, I have to give honor to the Lord first. My father was the founder of Jesse's Barber Shop. He was a Black man from Newbern, Alabama. As soon as he graduated from High School, he wanted to get out of there and he moved the same day as his graduation. My father moved to Pittsburgh, Pennsylvania in the early 1950s. He soon discovered that it wasn't much work there, so he joined the military. Shortly thereafter, the Korean Conflict broke out, but he was never engaged in combat. He stayed in Korea throughout the duration of his military career. After his completion and honorable discharge, he moved to Fort Wayne. He was hired at International Harvester. A manager confronted and asked him, what are you doing here? He told my dad he was 50 lbs. too light to work the job he was on and fired him.

My mom tried to persuade dad to go to barbering school, but he kept putting it off. He ended up going to barbering school and that turned out to be the best thing that ever happened to him. He and my mom moved to Indianapolis as he went to school and worked.

After graduation from Barbering School, my mom and dad moved back to Fort Wayne. He was soon employed by the late City Councilman John Nuckols for his first barbering job. He ran Councilman Nuckols Barber Shop so that Mr. Nuckols could spend more time working in the political arena. The arrangement worked out perfectly for the both of them.

My father ran the shop for a while, but he became aware of an old ice cream shop on Hanna Street at Brackenridge. He purchased the building in 1957 or 1958, and it became Jesse's Barber Shop and later Jesse & Son's Barber Shop. The shop went very well for him. He had 4 children. I was born in 1964. In 1967, he had a house built on the south side of Fort Wayne. This was very unusual for a barber and almost unheard of about Blacks of that time. A lot of people thought my father was a doctor or lawyer. When I told them he was a Barber, they wouldn't believe it. My father raised us while he worked in his barber shop. When the long hair of Afros became popular in the 1970s, that knocked him down for a few years, so my mom went to work and helped out.

I got involved in barbering business in the 1980s because my father's problems with sugar diabetes were getting worse. The business was flourishing and he said one day he will have to leave it. At this time I was a commercial artist working for a company in Indianapolis. It took me a while to decide to quit that job. I eventually resigned from my job and then enrolled in barbering school. I graduated and moved back to Fort Wayne to work with my dad in May of 1992.

It took me a while to make the decision to do this because my father, as Eric knows, was sometimes a very hard man to get along with because is was very opinionated. It took me a while to decide to work with him because I thought we would be bumping heads. Of course we did, but that's not what I gained from the experience. Our bumping heads is really nothing to think about.

Like I said, I started working there cutting hair in May of

1992. I got mad at my dad one Saturday because I had made so much money and I didn't realize how much money I could make barbering. It was phenomenal. In working in my dad's shop and learning from other Black barbers, because our clientele was primarily African American, was an invaluable experience. Learning from and listening to older Black men on how to raise your family, the importance of keeping your word and they taught me all about entrepreneurship.

So after cutting hair, I opened up another Barber Shop called Barber's on the Boulevard located at the corner of So. Anthony and Rudisill Blvd. I didn't cut there in the beginning, but I put three chairs in the facility and hired three Barbers, James Hopkins, Chris Cork and Harvest Higgins. They ran the shop and handled business very well. Then they moved on and opened their own shop. It's like a chain linked fence, you keep moving on. Of course you occasionally bump heads, but I admired them for what they did. Once they left, I moved in and cut hair there for a while until another gentleman named Jeff Hill came in to cut hair.

I then got an idea from one of my clients about another opening another business. So I started up called Technicom, a company where I provided telecommunications technicians to subcontract for other companies. The ideas for starting businesses all stemmed back to my father, Eric's father and brother and older Black men on how they were doing things and working their businesses. They were teaching me how to pass things on and even if you had a business and got rid of it, still passing on the legacy of getting another business started or at least the entrepreneurial thought process.

I've noticed that people put Fort Wayne down a lot. At times, there is not a lot to do here. I've been to different places around the world, but I always liked to come back to Fort Wayne. It's a good place to raise a family. You don't have too many problems here and it's been good for me. That's basically my story on how I got stated in business. I have to thank older Black men of Fort Wayne and I had to knock barriers down for myself.

You touched on several important points. You mentioned reluctance to work with your dad because your personalities may clash.

(Scott Williams): I never really knew my father that well because he was at work all the time, taking care of business. My mom raised us. My mom took care of the house business and when my dad came home, he was told what happened during the day. I wasn't afraid of my father, because it's not like he ever spanked me, in fact he only hit me twice in life. The spanking was needed at the time. But my father was a strong man and I tried not to make him mad at me. I just never tried to cause any problems. Looking back on my relationship with my father, the reason we may have clashed as adults was because I was Jesse Jr., just like my dad because the fruit doesn't fall far from the tree.

But one thing I can say about my father even though we clashed, my father respected me very much because of my family life. I married a young lady named Tamarra Wallace (Williams now) and we have 5 kids between us and none outside our family. You don't see that in a lot from Black families. If you do, usually more than the husband and wife are involved. When I was growing up, 5 kids in one family was a small family. Now if my wife and I walk down the street with our kids, people think it's a hoard of kids. But it's not. It shows how society is changing.

We have 5 kids and the oldest is 19 and the youngest is 12. So you know we're stair stepped. I don't mean to put any other parents down when I say this, but I will not even let my kids watch regular non-cabled TV without being monitored because of the shocking programming that's aired. The first Super Bowl I let my kids watch featured Janet Jackson at half-time when she had her wardrobe malfunction.

I'm not trying to block them from life, but society has changed so much too where the Village doesn't raise the child anymore. If I brought your child to the house because I was driving by and he was in the middle of the street and grabbed him and brought him home, now day's you will have to deal with an adult asking you what are you doing with my child. When I was coming up, the parent would be thanked for looking out for getting their kid out of harm's way. But getting back to my father, he respects me on how I raise my family.

When I was a kid, I hated getting hair cuts because it took so long. That's why I liked your father, he was known as "Fast Jesse."

(SW): He was about business. That was one thing about my dad. Whatever he did, he wanted to have an edge. Back when my dad began until presently, barbers aren't usually open on Mondays because of the union. My dad said, "why would you have a union when you're the owner and the worker?" It didn't make sense to him. So he didn't join the union and he cut hair on Mondays and made a killing financially.

But my father was fast. He could cut your hair in under 5 minutes. That fact was so well known, that when people came up from Alabama or other places from the south, they would make a bet. The bet was that my father would tell the person how fast he would get to them and If he was wrong, the haircut would be free. He never lost a bet.

Also in the 1960s, he always had a new car.

(SW): That's because how well barbering was going for him.

Did he ever get any negative backlash from Blacks about the frequency in his buying new cars?

(SW): No because at that time, things were different. Now, it seems that we're our own worst enemy. If someone sees you doing something positive or in someway prospering, it seems like they'll down grade you. They won't elevate or support what you're doing. But back in the early 1960s, whether you needed a hair cut of not, you did so to support a Black business. Successful Blacks were used as a testament to what other Blacks could do and become. Their success was admired and respected. Jealously and envy had not yet infiltrated the Black mindset.

My father was a flashy man. That's just how he was. The only negative thing people could say about my dad was that he was a very opinionated man. He was like, in the barber shop scene of the movie with Eddie Murphy and Arsenio Hall "Coming to America." A Black Barber Shop was a social gathering place, a place for financial help, Black community news and issue debate. We were located right next door to a church. More people would come to our shop for help and contributions than would go to the church. I'm not putting the church down, but that's the way it was. My father told me you have to step up and help. You may not be able to give all the time, but always try to help because it will come back to you.

You have 5 children. How do you control them?

(SW): I'm like my dad. Child abuse is child abuse. But there is also child rearing. When I was in school and you did something wrong, you got a swat. You didn't want your parents to find out because when you went home, you got another swat. So we did right. My kids, if they need a spanking, they'd get it. A lot of times we may go out to eat in a restaurant. People all the time would walk up to us and give me and my wife compliments. We would hear people remark, "they're so quiet and well behaved." That's because I raise my kids the way we were raised.

Whenever I see you and talk with you, you never seem to be stressed, frustrated or in anyway upset. You seem genuinely happy and content with your life. I've never heard you complain about your kids or speak ill of your wife. Tell me about Mrs. Williams.

(SW): I'm the Titanic and she's the rudder. The man has the last say-so in the house. Not "man", but a good Christian based man. I've done my wrongs, the Lord knows that. But I'm trying to be right and my wife see's that. I've had a lot of money in my hands from the different businesses that I've had. I've had money, lost it and gained it back again. And I know I'll have more, kind of like Job in the Bible. It's like living an adventure. If I have an idea, I speak with my wife about it. She gives me her insights and I use her input for my final decision. It may not always be what she said, but believe me it's in the back of my head what she said.

Some people think we're wealthy. We are wealthy with love and we're wealthy with our family. One day the Lord said "you're going to be wealthy." Then he woke me up and said go look in the other room where your kids are asleep. He said "that's your wealth." You take care of them and that's all you'll ever need.

Scott with dad, the late Jesse Williams

KEKIONGA BLACKS' War on HIS-Story & Slave Mentality

Interview with Mrs. Eauleen Chapman,
1st Black Female Cheerleader of
Central High School and in the history of
Fort Wayne Community High Schools

Hackley: Tell us about your transition from Alabama to Fort Wayne.

Eauleen Chapman (EC): When my family moved to Fort Wayne, I already had a lot of relatives here and we lived in very close proximity to each. So It was like a family reunion when we got here. My relatives and I all attended Harmar School. There was two blocks between home and school. I would engage with family members about everyday.

KEKIONGA BLACKS' War on HIS-Story & Slave Mentality

In Alabama, we lived on a farm. We were surrounded by chickens, pigs and all kind of different fruits. It was segregated. We lived 18 miles from town. It was just us out there in the country until we went to town on Saturday. In town, we had certain areas where we could sit. We had a block in town were some of the seats were for Whites and some seats were where Blacks could sit.

As you look back, did it seem odd that Blacks could only sit in assigned areas?

(EC): No it didn't. It was the norm and that's what we did. We never thought any other way. That's all we knew.

Did you have relationships with Whites outside of the farm?

(EC): We didn't have anything to do with Whites in Alabama. The only time we saw Whites was when we went to the store in town and when the mail carrier delivered our mail. The mail carrier was very nice and would offer to take us into town if we had to go for something during a week. We knew what we could do and what we couldn't do. We couldn't use their bathrooms. When we came to Fort Wayne, it was all together different. We used the same bathrooms and went to the same schools.

Were there any restrictions on Blacks in Fort Wayne?

(EC): Oh yes. There were restrictions on where you could eat. When I first moved here, there were certain counters where Blacks could stand and eat and the White people could sit down and eat. At Murphy's and other dime stores downtown that had restaurants and a stand-up bar, that's where the Blacks could eat. Standing up to eat was ok with us because we were use to it. We basically accepted whatever was offered to us.

At what age did your spirit of independence start to emerge?

(EC): Maybe at the age of 12 or 13, I started to notice that things were wrong and we were not going to accept business as usual. By that time they were starting to let us do a little bit more. We could now go downtown to Murphy's and eat while sitting down. They may not wait on us for 15 or 20 minutes, but we could still sit there. Then they would finally come around and wait on us.

What were your earliest memories of socializing with White people in Fort Wayne?

KEKIONGA BLACKS' War on HIS-Story & Slave Mentality

(EC): When we first started socializing with Whites, we became friends. When we went to high school, they were a little different and they treated us differently from the business establishments. We could be friends and some would even come to your house. I went to some of their houses and some of their families were ok with that. Not many, but a few and we did it. It was a little different. My father always thought we may get hurt if we went to their homes, so we had to go without him knowing it. We weren't being defiant, we were just curious.

At Central in 1952, I became the first Black cheerleader in the history of Fort Wayne Community Schools. I didn't really face any opposition. Central and most of the Fort Wayne schools only had boy cheerleaders at that time. So a bunch of us girls decided to go out and I was selected to be a cheerleader.

I've kind of always been independently minded. I did accomplish most of my goals because I would stick with it if I wanted to do something. I would do pretty much what I wanted, regardless of what anyone had to say. Most of my high school teachers were pretty much lenient in letting us do what we wanted to do.

Our teachers cared about us and they wanted us to learn. They projected to us that we had to learn and if we didn't, we would get suspended. I had the kind of parents that, if I got in trouble in school, I would be reprimanded at home. So I had to keep my grades up.

In the era of my cheerleading, the dominant athletes were Tom Knox, Eugene Barksdale and Jim Blevins come to mind. Tom Knox was a terrific basketball player, but very low keyed. They all came along after Johnny Bright.

In 1955, during the Rosa Parks Montgomery Bus Boycott, we felt the ramifications here because there were a lot of things that Blacks were not allowed to do in Fort Wayne. Blacks could only live in certain areas and that went on for many years. As far as I could see, the Blacks here were very receptive of Martin Luther King and the Civil Rights Movement. Because if you ever quit pushing for change for the better, it will never happen. Martin Luther King was one who would not quit. We realized that we needed the rights Dr. King was pushing and fighting for.

I worked for Northern Indiana Public Service Company (NIPSCO) downtown in the office. Myself and Jamila Churchill were hired the same day and were the first two Blacks hired by NIPSCO. At the time, they had a Black elevator operator. Each time we would get on the elevator, she would always start doing her nails or something and never spoke to us the whole time we were there.

Why do Blacks seem to have a problem with Blacks who have better jobs?

(EC): I could never really understand that because I always tried to help people get positions at NIPSCO once I got hired. I also worked for the City for a number of years and I got quite a few people hired by the City of Fort Wayne. That was the first thing I started to do. I would basically recruit Blacks who I thought would qualify to come in and apply. In the early 1980s, I was the secretary for Mayor Win Moses. Then I worked in voter registration, for the license bureau and I had been around politics for quite a while.

When you worked for Mayor Moses, I noticed how easily you maneuvered in that environment. Why didn't you ever enter politics as a candidate?

(EC): I had planned all my life to run for public office. I co-hosted Bobby Kennedy's headquarters when he ran for president and visited Fort Wayne. All of my life, I had wanted to be a politician. Then I had a child in 1969 that was disabled. The doctors told me she was going to live for two years. She lived 42 years. I still worked, participated in neighborhood and church activities, but I had no time to devote to politics and I wouldn't devote time away from my daughter.

Were you present at the 1987 Win Moses vs. Paul Helmke debate at True Love Baptist Church?

(EC): Yes I was there.

I videotaped it and still have it. It was the most awesome debate performance in recorded Fort Wayne history where two White Mayoral candidates with fiery laser focus in their eyes and were spitting thunder and lightening as they expressed sincerity in competing for the vote of Fort Wayne Black People. I don't think we will ever see such a spectacle again and I don't think anyone will ever care about Black people to that magnitude ever again.

(EC): I think Win Moses was the best politician that I have ever been around. And Paul Helmke is a very, very nice fellow and I knew him very well. Whatever they wanted to say, they would say and they would go all out for what they wanted to do.

Why don't people seem to care anymore about Blacks?

(EC): Because all they want to do is to get in office. They'll look you in the face and tell a lie and just keep going. They don't care. Number one, they try to keep Blacks from the voting booths. In order to register to vote, you need a picture ID. They're just not interested anymore in the concerns of Black people.

How do you feel when a Black person tells you they have never voted and don't intend to because it makes no difference anyway?

(EC): I get very, very upset. Many people have told me that. I have let them know what they should do in order to help themselves. If they don't get out there and vote, we'll never get anyplace. And I have good friends who have never voted.

Why have you never moved away from the inner city?

I think that I do a lot of things that people don't do for Blacks. I help the neighborhood. I help sick people, old people, disabled people and I help anyone I can. I like to live around my people because I'm comfortable here.

How did you meet your husband James?

(EC): I had a sister who was in his brother Link Chapman's wedding. We met then. He soon after went away and spent two years in Korea. When he returned, we got started again, got married and had a family. It's been 57 years now.

I have been working many years trying to document the Chapman family story. Why is it that your husband and his 8 brothers have the ability to fix, build or grow anything?

(EC): As far as I can see, my husband's father died when he was 1 year old. A couple of the brothers were old enough to be out on their own. But their mother instilled into them that they had to do something to be something. Five or six of them had their own businesses and they did well in their businesses. From what I've heard from the brothers who were in business, they weren't too particular about working for other people because they wanted to get out on their own.

Link built his building, a huge building down on Creighton and his kids are still running it. Another brother Elvin founded Chapman Auto Diagnostic Services on Eliza Street and his son Larry is currently running it. It's not they didn't want to take orders from other people. They felt they could be a better asset to their families and the Black community if they had their own businesses.

Looking back over the years, when was Fort Wayne's Black community strong and when did it start to unravel?

(EC): That's hard to say because in the 1960s things seemed to be going well and in the 1980s things stopped. John Nuckols was a man who really had Fort Wayne going. To me he was probably the most talented Black political leader we've had and he did a lot for Black people. Then Cletus Edmonds came along. Then after that, a lot of them worked, but they didn't have any help. Today's people are just not interested anymore. You need money to do things. A lot of us want to use our money on things that we can benefit from today. Maybe it takes five years to start making money from a business venture and many Blacks don't want to do this. They can't wait on the time it takes to grow a business. If they can't make money today or tomorrow, they won't do it.

James and Eualeen Chapman

KEKIONGA BLACKS' War on HIS-Story & Slave Mentality

I would now like to present Rev. Charles Martin and ask him to speak on how he lifted himself up by his own bootstraps, from G.E.D to Masters Degree

Thank you very much, Mr. Hackley.

I'm Rev. Charles Martin and I would like to share with you my personal experience in the hope that through the illustration of my life someone may gleam some information that would contribute to their life and help them to see that it is possible to overcome difficult and challenging situations in life.

I am one of eleven children who was victimized by the murder of my father in a small Alabama town called Centerville. A so called friend murdered him. I do not remember much about my father, but I do know that he brought his paycheck home, at least enough of it to feed his children and pay the rent. I know that's better stewardship than many of the children at the facility where I work. I am a counselor at a prison in Fort Wayne for juveniles. Many of the children there have not seen or heard from their parents in six to twenty four months.

By the time I was four years old, my father was dead. All he left behind was a life of difficult challenges, pain and a poverty stricken family. But that didn't stop mom. She packed our bags and moved the 11 of us here to Fort Wayne. Mom did her best, but all of us did not survive.

First my sister died, then my brother and then finally mom. But strangely enough, I never did blame God. I just recall when I needed someone, he was always there. But to think about the odds of staying alive in the unfortunate environment of the poor class and coming out educated, tears trickle from my eyes. Because I realize that not only did God keep me in his providential care, but he kept me in the protective custody of his strong hands.

I dropped out of Central High School in the 12th grade, but some four or five years later I went back and obtained a G.E.D. What encouraged me to do that is the recommendation of the people I associated with. I was working as a short order cook at IPFW. One of the nurses there that I went to when I was ill, recommended that I go talk to a guidance counselor.

From there, he encouraged me to enroll in a two year program called Mental Health Technology. I enrolled in that program and was satisfied with being in that program because it helped me to understand some of the things that were occurring within me psychologically.

After the completion of that program, with a lot of fear and intimidation I enrolled in a Bachelors Degree program. I completed that program while working two jobs. Then I went on and enrolled in a Masters Degree program at Ball State University. I complete that program and went to work for the Fort Wayne State Developmental Center. I started of as a direct care worker and I was soon elevated to the position of Director.

In my later years, I decided that being in administration was not satisfying to me. So I transferred to my current job and I now work as a counselor with the teenagers that I mentioned to you earlier.

Thank you Mr. Hackley.

KEKIONGA BLACKS' *War on HIS-Story & Slave Mentality*

I would like to introduce to you a courageous Fort Wayne woman who has a message of enlightenment for everyone struggling with an addiction. At this time, I would like to introduce Ms. Nanette Thomas.

My name is Nanette Thomas and I am a recovering addict. I have over 20 years of sobriety under my belt. It has been an on going battle. I've been through quite a few things in my life that took me down that road. I'm glad to say I'm sober now.

One of the things I've been through in life that led me down the road of drugs happened when I turned 21. I thought I would have some fun, so I took my first drink and I smoked my first joint. Then I moved to Fort Wayne and I was going through some hard times.

I still smoked bud, but a friend and I started smoking primo. Primo took me down the road to smoke crack cocaine. But like I said. I've been sober for 20 years and it has been an on going battle. I've recovered a couple of times and relapsed a couple of times. The one thing that made me really take my sobriety seriously was that wanted my life back because I had changed. I had not been the mother that I had always use to be. My son use to be able to trust me when I told him something. Then things just totally changed, meaning that he could no longer trust me.

He'd sometimes have to come find me. I was a working woman, but on my weekends I would sometime disappear and he wouldn't see me again for two or three days later. But the thing that really turned my life around was one day I came home after being on one of my binges and I had on white clothes when I had gone to work. When I came home, my clothes were totally a dingy gray, close to being black. I was so ashamed that I had my mom take my son to my neighbors house so I could go home and change clothes. Then I remembered that I asked her for 75 cents for bus fare so I could go turn myself in to a rehab center in order to get my life back. My mom didn't realize I was on drugs.

I have accomplished so much since I turned my life around. Since then, my mom has gone through heart surgery and I had to be strong for her and be there for her. I know that without my sobriety, I could not have done these things. I have helped my son by being a good influence for him. He has graduated from college and now he's a productive citizen in Indianapolis and now I have grandchildren that I can be proud of.

The things I do now, I can say that my higher power and my sobriety are what took me to the level of where I am now. I know there is nothing that I cannot accomplish if I really want too. I say no to drugs every day and I hope that one day everyone who is addicted to drugs will have their lives turn out the way mine has, and maybe I'll be the one who helped you. I guess that's all I have to say for now. I'm kind of nervous right now and I'm sorry.

I'm sure this is a very difficult subject for you talk about. What point is not being communicated to people who still want to smoke crack for the first time?

(NT) That it can take you no where but down. You have two places where you can end up, in prison or dead. And it's your choice. You just have to want a better life and it's always some-one who can help you. I am willing to be anyone's sponsor if they needed help. When I help someone, it helps me in my sobriety to be strong.

Can you be a recreational crack smoker or are you addicted and in denial?

(NT) You cannot be a recreational smoker with crack cocaine be-cause I was under the same impression. When I first turned myself into rehab, I thought that since I didn't smoke crack 24/7 and that I didn't get real thin, looking rugged and all that, that I wasn't an addict. But it took me going to rehab to find out that just like there's a weekend alcoholic, there's a weekend addict. When it's crack cocaine, it's not how many times a day you do it, or how often you do it, it's when you do it you lose control. You are not going to quit smoking until your money is gone and you have no other way to get high.

Why can't you be as persuasive when on crack cocaine as when you're sober?

(NT) With crack cocaine addiction, if someone presents or sells them self in a certain way when they're high, when they're sober they can do the same thing, but they don't have the gumption to do so. "Being honest" for me is important because with my sobriety comes honesty. I had lost that when I became an addict. Like I said, I wasn't honest with my son. I would disappoint him and I had disappointed my mom. But when I got my sobriety back, that's why it's so important for me to be a truthful and honest person. When I was a drug addict, all the truthfulness and honesty was gone.

No matter how much you love someone like I love my mom and son with all my heart. But I couldn't become sober because I love them. I had to become sober because I love myself. I remember the woman who saved my life, she's dead now, she happened to relapse. She was a heroine addict. She and my higher power saved my live. That's why I would love to give back what she gave to me. With her help and my wanting to help myself and have a better life and be the kind of person that I had always been, I had to let them know I needed help because I had lost control of my life and I wanted my life back.

I remember when I first went to detoxification. At the detox, they let you out in three days. They told me there were no openings in their program, but I begged them. I told them I can't leave here because if you let me leave here now, it will be like I haven't done anything to get better. I'll be right back in the situation that I was in when I came here. They let me stay and be part of their program and get my life back. I asked the lady to take me home to get my clothes, because I didn't even want to go home by myself. And they gave me my life back.

Thank you for listening.

Interview with the late Corporal Charles A. Jones, Retired United States Marine Corps {1947~2013}

Why did you originally join the Marine Corps?

(Charles Jones): I volunteered on March 3, 1965. I ran track at Central High School and during my senior year I became ineligible. So I joined the Marines.

How soon afterwards were you assigned to Viet Nam?
(Jones): I arrived first arrived in Viet Nam on September 5, 1965.

When you were going through basic training, was it a good experience for you?
(Jones): It was a great experience. It taught me survival techniques, and gave me a military mindset. It taught self-discipline and respect for authority. All in all, it was a good experience.

KEKIONGA BLACKS' War on HIS-Story & Slave Mentality

Once you get your expert training as a Marine, you have a lot of military confidence. You can think for yourself. You can lead if the situation arises where your platoon sergeant or squad leader gets killed. You can take his place and perform his function. It was a good leadership experience.

What was your motivation for joining the Marines?
Initially I wanted to further my sports career through special services where I could play football, basketball and run track. That was my initial idea. But after being in the Marine Corps you find out that everyone is a rifleman. A cook is a rifleman. It's a very militaristic organization. One of the mottos is, "first to fight" and it's strictly about combat and you fighting the wars of our country.

Were you tuned in to the political side as to why we were there? Or were you more tuned in to what you had to do to protect yourself in a war zone?
I was more concerned with what I had to do in a war zone. Initially all your instincts take over and it's all about survival. I had no political consensus. You have a military outlook on everything. You think about saving your partner or buddy as they say. You become tight with individuals in a unique way. That's all you think about. Making sure he doesn't get killed. Making sure you do your job. Making sure he does his job and you become a tight group of Marines.

Tell me about your first experience after hearing a bullet whizzing by your head.
It was a sudden shock of reality because you're never really totally prepared for war until you're in an actual firefight or combat situation. When I heard the bullets going around my head, my mind said "this is it." This is what you've been trained for. That's what kept going through my mind. Then automatically your training takes over. When you hear bullets, you hit the ground. Then you put a bullet in your chamber, try to find the enemy and return fire. Your training takes over.

How soon did you get into your first life or death battle?
It was on October 14th or 15th of 1965 on Hill 22. We were on an outpost when 243 Marines were killed on that day. It was the 1st Battalion, 1st Marines Alpha Company. We got hit in broad daylight which was rare. Whenever you get hit in broad daylight in Viet Nam, you're usually out numbered three or four to They would have never taken us on when the numbers were even. They ran us

off the hill until we got reinforcements from Charley company. We fought them hand to hand and drove them back into the jungle and took the hill back. It was about a six hour battle.

How did the battle begin?
This was a regular day, even during a war. We were getting chow, loading our magazines, getting ready for a night ambush or patrols around Hill 22. Then they attacked us with 60mm mortars and heavy machine gunfire. The gunfire pent everyone down and that's when they overran the Hill with AK47s. We killed a lot of them but they jumped in the hole with one of the sergeants and blew him up with a satchel charge of C4. There was a lot of hand to hand fighting.

Did you engage in hand to hand fighting yourself?
Well yes. When they overtook the hill, the enemy actually took and occupied the fighting holes we had. They occupied our position. Me and Sgt. Keys a 6th degree Black Belt, who was my ITR instructor at camp Geiger in California, we went into the fighting holes that the enemy now occupied and took them on in hand to hand combat. We took the positions back from them. We had instructors in boot camp to teach us hand to hand combat training, karate classes and bayonet training. In a conflict, the training takes over. There's a lot said about marines, but we have the best training in the world.

What was your worst War experience?
The night before the battle, I talked with my Lieutenant before he was killed in battle the next day. He came over to my fox hole the night before the battle and he said he had a premonition. He said "Jonesy, I think I'm going to get it". I said sir, that's a bad thing to tell your point man because I might lose my life trying to save your life. I wish you hadn't told me that. He was killed after we took back Hill 22 and we went down to sweep the area. The enemy ambushed us again at the river. The Lieutenant led the charge after the enemy and he chased them into a minefield. He was killed instantly when he stepped on a landmine and was shot 4 times in the chest by an AK47. I saw him when he was hit. He was no more than 5 meters in away from me. He took the leadership and they killed him. That was really hard for me take. We called in for reinforcements and a helicopter to take him back to the rear echelon hospital. It was really traumatic. Squad leader Sgt. Braderhurst and I walked into the minefield, took our rifles and made a sling and placed the Lieutenant's body on it and waited for

the helicopter to arrive. That was really an intense and prolonged combat experience.

You mentioned you were a point man. That's the most dangerous position to be in, isn't it?
Yes, I was a point man all the time I was there for 1st battalion, 1st Marines. On my first tour of duty I spent 13 months in Viet Nam. It was dangerous, but once you know what you're doing and you feel like you know what you're doing and you engage the enemy and you understand that if you see him before he sees you, if you can get your squad or platoon in position and you've got the fastest trigger finger, you'll win the battle for that day. You've got to be sharp. You've got to know what you're doing and after a while it becomes a job and you get good at what you do. And it all goes back to our training.

Were most of the Black guys point men?
There was a disproportionate number of African Americans in Viet Nam. A disproportionate number in the different platoons. It depended on how good of a Marine you were, how well trained you were and If you went to gorilla warfare school. Being in the Marine Corps was similar to being in college. You go to classes every day, you learn how to read a compass and a map. You learn about the enemy and his equipment. You learn the specs of the AK47 that has a clip capacity of 30 rounds. We had 20 clip capacity in the M14. You know if you are engaged in a firefight with the enemy, you know he has more ammo. He has 10 more rounds per clip. So you've got top make your rounds count. If you were trained well, usually things worked out in your favor.

Did you experience any anti-American propaganda from the enemy?
At times Hanoi Hanna would speak over the radio and say why don't you lay down your weapons Black Marines. The Imperialist country of America has you over here killing 3rd world people. The propaganda was horrific. The effort was also impacted by the protestors in the United States of America. Protestors were going around the country talking about the Marines, the Army Airborne. It was the first war the American people were not behind and for. Everyone was for WWI and WWII. Korea was more of a forbidden war and not too much was said about it. But the Viet Nam propaganda was horrific by the Chinese communists and Russians. They did a great job on the American public. If you got into a fight and you know me, but I cheer for the other person that you're fight-

ing, you're going to say, "what's wrong with Charles? I thought he was my friend." It had a demoralizing aspect psychologically. The same kind of analogy can be applied to the propaganda machines of American protestors and the communists.

Once you returned to the United States, did you have any violent or inappropriate post battle disorders?
Not anything violent. But after that much time spent in a jungle where it's kill or be killed, you have night sweats, nightmares and reflections on a host of traumatic experiences that you relive. I had these issues, but I adjusted. I had a lot of help from WWII and Korean War Veterans. This 10 year battle was the longest "war" in US history.

What can be done today to help Viet Nam and all veterans?
The veteran's representatives of city, county, state and federal governments need to be compassionate people who understand the homelessness, psychiatric displacement and nervous conditions. They need to more aggressively go into the field. If veterans are homeless and sleeping under bridges, go under the bridges or where ever they are. There needs to be a continual outreach of outgoing compassion. Let the veterans know they are loved and want to be cared for by the American people. In this way they can be cared for and be reintegrated back into the system for help, instead of a veteran being all alone, to struggle with their personal issues on the street, the best way they can.

Eric Hackley interviewing Retired Cpl. Charles Jones
KEKIONGA BLACKS' War on HIS-Story & Slave Mentality

Interview with Bob Hawkins, Owner
HAWKINS HOUSE of *FISH* & RESTAURANT
at 2619 WEISSER PARK AVE
(260) 456 2040
At the Corner of Pontiac and Weisser Park St. since 1974.

Bob Hawkins, Restaurateur: Learned Work Ethic From Cotton Field

KEKIONGA BLACKS' War on HIS-Story & Slave Mentality

Never Be a Quitter: A Bob Hawkins Narrative

Everyone in my community was Black and my dad was like an overseer. When the White property owners needed someone to pick peanuts, peaches, chop cotton or pick cotton, my dad would get a group of people together and the plantation owner would come with a truck and there would be 30 to 40 of us waiting to be picked up to go to various fields through out the community to do whatever jobs needed to be done.

I can remember waking up on my mother's cotton sack and she would tell me to get on the other side of the row and say, "baby help mama pick some cotton." I know I wasn't five yet because I would always hold up five fingers and she would tell me I wasn't five yet. I would ask her the question of when would I be five? Mom said, "you have to wait until Santa Clause comes and that's when you'll be five. My birthday was on Christmas.

We didn't really interact with Whites that much. After we worked all week in the fields, on Saturday we would go into town to the store. This is when we would interact with them. As a kid, I would get a RC Cola, peanuts, ice cream, things like that as a reward for picking cotton all week. As far as White people, we would see them in the store, look at them or we would have to get off the path for them.

As a child, I didn't realize the proper code of conduct for Blacks. My mom did. She would tell me to watch my manners and watch my place, things of that nature so that I wouldn't create a problem or cause controversy with a White person. Basically at that time of our history, Black people did not want to cause any problems. Blacks couldn't dispute anything. Whatever a White person would say is the law. Being put in jail or being fined would keep you out of the field and from earning income for your family. That's why you always stayed in line. You learned that lesson as a small child.

When I came to Fort Wayne in the late 1940s, still relatively young, I came out of an all Black community, I was heart broken because all my friends who I went to school with, were still in Arkansas. Going to a mixed Harmar grade school was new to me. In Arkansas, all my teachers, the kids in school and everyone in my community were Black. Pine City was segregated. I never had a White teacher until I came to Fort Wayne and this was my first time being around Whites on a daily basis. I never really talked to a White person until I came to Fort Wayne.

KEKIONGA BLACKS' War on HIS-Story & Slave Mentality

Being a small child in Arkansas, I was protected from insults and put downs. I remember getting into a fight at Harmar when a White boy called me a nigger. It didn't mean anything to me because that was the first time I had heard it. I didn't know what the word meant. But a friend of mine named James Fowlkes, we called him Pete, I was about 11 at the time and Pete said, "you can't let him get away with that." I said, get away with what? "That word he called you." It's just a word to me. But then I found out it was a racial put down.

That's how I learned about racial prejudice and the word nigger, right here in Fort Wayne. Racial prejudice and the n-word were I'm sure expressed in Arkansas, but as a small kid, I was protected and wasn't exposed directly to it. But even at picnics and other associations when large groups of Black people would get together in Arkansas, we never argued or called each other names like that. We would have disputes, but I never heard that word.

For fun we would play baseball, have foot races, shoot marbles and play hide-and-go-seek. I think you grew up faster in the south because you had horses and various forms of live stocks. You would bet a kid your horse could out run his horse. At Harmar, we had physical education classes. During those classes, we had a teacher named Pete Barley and we had foot races. He would pair up boys of the same size and have us race 50 yards. That's how I got interested in track. There were guys like Tharnell Hollins, John Kelso, George Middleton, Eddie Russell, Glen West and others who went on to be great athletes at Central, all those guys were at Harmar. And we raced against each other.

Between Harmar and James H. Smart which was across the tracks, during the major track meets and tournaments, we "Black schools" became the major athletic forces among the Fort Wayne grade schools. However, there was one White school that did pretty well and that was Forest Park. But all the other schools were no competition for us. James H. Smart had I believe, Frank Smith and Earl Coker. Back then, a lot of those guys lived across the tracks and I lived around Eliza Street and you really didn't affiliate with the guys on the other side of town. The only time I really knew them was at track meets and we weren't really friends, but Frank Smith was pretty fast. I didn't know the people from Westfield either. We didn't become friends until we attended Central High School.

KEKIONGA BLACKS' War on HIS-Story & Slave Mentality

I didn't get any major athletic recognition until I got to Central. I was always a small, skinny kid. George Middleton, John Kelso, Frank Smith, Tharnell Hollins and Eddie Russell were all bigger and faster than me in the 100 and 220 yard dashes. I weighed about 114 lbs. when I was 14 years old and George Middleton was a lot more muscular. When we had gym classes at Central, we had further distances to run than over at Harmar. Now we had the 440, half-mile, mile and even cross country which was 2 miles.

That's when I found out that after a quarter mile, those guys who could out run me in the sprints, I could hold my own from a quarter mile and longer. That's when I became a standout because I was out running those guys. I became a standout at Central because as a miler, I was beating White guys. Back then, no Black kids were running distances, they were sprinters. If you weren't a sprinter, you basically weren't on the team. We had hard track practices. We would run from Lewis St. to Clinton, to Rudisill, to Lafayette back to Central, then I would go to work.

My success was due to my coaching and the recognition I was getting from doing well athletically. Also I wasn't doing drugs, smoking or drinking. Others were doing that. They would have a Cigarette or two. As you know if you run distance, you need lung capacity to do that. But you weren't cool if you didn't have a pack of cigarettes rolled up in your short sleeve shirt. Once I took a puff or two off a cigarette and I had a race the next day and I didn't have the wind and I noticed that. I didn't get first. I found out there was more recognition and notoriety if I won the race. So that's deterred me from smoking, using drugs and alcohol.

When we would go to track meets, we would go in a truck. Since I was a primary runner, the coach Pete Williams would have me ride up front with him so we could map out strategy. He would tell me who the fastest was from that school. He would tell me I was a natural and talk about the my stride saying to me, "Hawkins, you know running is just like life." I said but Pete, I'm the only Black kid running distance. Black guys don't run distance, they're sprinters. Pete said, "Hawkins, can you out run Kelso, Hollins or Russell? You can't out run any of those kids. Who can you out run as a sprinter?" He said, "you're a distance runner."

I would tell coach, but I get tired. "Hawkins, that other kid gets tired too. That's the way life is, you can't be a quitter. There are going to be times when you're out of school, when you're married with a family, and you may not want to go to work. It may be cold outside and if you start quitting early in life, you'll always be a quitter. Never be a quitter." He would tell me that over and over and it stuck with me. He was a great influence.

My dad was also a great influence in my athletic success. I had a mom and dad who were both together at home. My dad would often come by our track on Lewis Street. I would see him standing at the fence watching us practice. I didn't let anyone beat me in front of my dad. When he saw someone beat me he would say, "boy I thought you could run. You let that little kid beat you." He would say something like that and I didn't want to be embarrassed.

My biggest achievements at Central were breaking the half-mile and mile records of Bob and Chuck Kirtz. They were two White guys who were brothers. I broke both of their records as a sophomore. Also in getting my cross country sweater as a sophomore. Most didn't get theirs until they were juniors or seniors because you had to accumulate so many points.

I remember once when Central had never won a Sectional cross country meet and it was going to take place at Franke Park. We had a bunch of Black guys and a few Whites on our Cross Country team. Back then North Side was dominant and cross country was about all white sport. Rollie Chambers was the track coach at North Side. I can remember Pete Williams telling us that Rollie Chambers said, "he wouldn't have a bunch of niggers on his track team because they were a bunch of quitters. If they got tired, they didn't have any heart, they would quit".

In knowing Rollie Chambers, he probably said that. But I also wonder if that was a tactic that Pete Williams used on us to get us fired up. But it happened that North Side didn't win that Sectional meet, we did. That was the first time Central beat North Side and we won the Sectional Cross Country meet. I have a picture of myself running against Ewing, who was a standout at North Side and I beat him. In fact, I came in first place in that race.

My competitive nature came from when I was a kid in those long, hot Arkansas days in the field where you couldn't quit. You couldn't say, I'm tired, I want a bologna sandwich, some water or anything that. That was not inbred in me as a kid.

How did you get interested in Karate?
(Bob): There was a young lady I was associated with who was

about 5' 5" and about 125 lbs. She was attending a Karate School and she always wanted to practice on someone. Every time I saw her, she wanted to practice a block, a move or she wanted me to hold her in a headlock or something. Naturally, I was much bigger and stronger than she was but I noticed as time went on, she became a little more wirery. She was harder to hold or put into restraint and keep her there because she could always get out. She would tell me, Bob, "you're really fast and strong for your size. If you got into this, you'd really be good at it." That's how I really got into it. I just happened to notice how quick and strong she was getting. This chapter happened in the early 1970s when I was an adult.

There were two primary schools in Fort Wayne that I was looking at to join, Robert Bowles and Parker Shelton. Both these gentlemen had been National Champions. Mr. Bowles was a National Champion in weapons and he was about 5' 8". Mr. Shelton was about 5'11 or 6 foot at 250 lbs. At that time I was about 6 foot, 170 lbs. He was a National Champion in Kumite. So I figured, if I had a weapon, I didn't need karate. The way I looked at it, karate was using your feet and hands, so Mr. Shelton was a 6 time National Champion, so I decided to go with him to study in 1972 and that's what I did.

I went there primarily to stay in shape. I always stayed in shape after I graduated high school with push-ups and sit-ups, exercises of that nature. And when I went to his school, it was primarily kids there. I was the only adult. The next oldest person was 13. Anytime Mr. Sheldon wanted to do a demonstration, he would pick me because I was his size. So basically I was getting private lessons with more hands on in working with the instructor. I played the role of the oki or dummy so I had hands on training and that's how my talent and ability evolved.

I had a chance to fight some guys who eventually became national champions. One was Ross Scott out of Kokomo, Indiana. Glenn Keeney was his teacher. Glenn Keeney, Parker Shelton and all the Masters knew each other pretty well. A lot of times, they would bring their students to your dojo and you would take your students to their dojo to have inner dojo competitions. I can say this about Mr. Shelton, I was the only Black who started there. There were some other Black students who came later, but I can truthfully say, he showed no prejudice or anything of that nature.

KEKIONGA BLACKS' War on HIS-Story & Slave Mentality

I started out like everyone else as a White belt. In Fort Wayne, I rose to a 1st degree Brown Belt. When you first get a Brown Belt under the Shorin-Ryu style, you're 3rd degree. It kind of backward. You start out as a 3rd degree, then a 2nd degree and when you're beginning to test for Black, you're 1st degree. I was recommended four years after I started to go for my Black Belt, but I never did.

I didn't reach my Black Belt until International Harvester closed down and I moved to Ohio to work at Navistar International. While sitting around the house in the evening with nothing to do, I met some guys at work and they told me about a Karate School there in Urbana, Ohio, so I decided I would check it out. I stood there and watched the guys and the Brown belts that I saw at that school, I noticed that Indiana Karate was a lot more intense. That's how I kind of arrived. I started going to that school and started beating the Brown Belts because when you took Karate under Mr. Shelton, by me being as large as he was, he didn't hold back. So I was taught well at the Shelton School and I learned a lot.

If you beat the Brown Belts, they'll put you with a Black Belt for the overall tournament champion. I was a heavy weight at the time weighing 195 lbs. So they put me in with a Black Belt and I beat him. After I knocked him down a couple of times and this guy was a 3rd or 4th degree Black Belt they said, "where did this guy come from?" I told them I came out of Indiana. They said they wanted to test me and move me along. They said, "at his skill level, he shouldn't be a Brown Belt." Basically, if you're a Brown Belt and you beat a Black Belt, that's not good for the Black Belt you beat. It basically embarrasses their system. So I was tested over there for my Black Belt and got it in 1990.

How did you manage running a restaurant in Fort Wayne, working full time for Navistar International in Ohio and earning your Black Belt all at the same time?

(Bob): I was fortunate enough to have 6 sisters and we were a close knit family. My mother was a head cook and kind of ran things at one of the elite restaurants here in Fort Wayne, Bob Hadley's Trolley Bar. Her management skill was kind of passed down. My sister worked for the Gerber House Restaurant and my brother and Dave (who eventually founded Wendy's) cooked at Colonel Sanders.

When I first began the restaurant, I was working alone and

would open on Thursday, because that's when I weekly came back to town, thru Saturday. Then my sisters Willie Mae Hendricks and Georgia Butler said, while you're working in Ohio, we're not really doing anything. We can come down and run it. That's how I managed the restaurant. And my Karate classes were on Mondays and Wednesdays after work from 6:00 to 9:00 pm.

When you come out of a cotton field buddy, I want to tell you that I don't believe there's anything you can't do because *that is* manual labor. It wasn't like you going to work at 7:00 or 8:00 in the morning and worked until 3:00 in the evening because that's what you do in a factory. In a cotton field, you work from sun-up, to sun-down. That's 5:00 or 6:00 in the morning to 7 or 8:00 at night during the summer months. Once that work regiment was instilled in you as a child, that's basically your work ethic. So working at Navistar International was child's play for me compared with the work to which I had become accustomed.

Before I went to International Harvester, I had other jobs. I worked on car lots, washed windows and I worked at Parkview Hospital. I also worked at the Van Orman Hotel Supper Club where I went to work at 4:00 in the morning and on the way to work, I had to go to Westfield and pick up 4 or 5 guys.

I worked in the kitchen washing pots and pans and then became a short order cook. All this was right out of high school at 17 and 18 years old. When I got off work at 3:00, I'd be over parking trucks at 4:00 in the afternoon until 10 or 11:00 at night. So to me at that time, anyone who didn't have two jobs was lazy because I had been use to working in the cotton field all day from sun-up to sun-down.

The kids today don't have a good work ethnic in terms of stick-to-ativeness. There is an old saying, "you have to crawl before you walk". They don't have any of that. Everyone is looking for a hand-out, they don't want to work and earn it like I did. The problems of drugs and violence, I think those start at home. I went to school with a girl who had a kid at 14 years old and yes you can say it was kids having kids. But her kid, to my knowledge never went to jail and today he is a professional.

So I think it goes back to the parents and also today's laws. When I was in school and you did something wrong, you were chastised and punished through the power of fear. Now today's educators and psychologists are saying that damages a kid. I never went go to prison or jail. I don't consider myself being damaged. But I do know if you don't put fear in a child, you don't get the respect later on. So if I did something out of line, I knew what would happen to me.

A lot of times that person who saw me do something wrong would discipline me. We don't have that now. If that happens today, they want to sue that person. Once a child knows nothing will happen to them regardless of what they did, you can't control them. If you can't control them, how will you get them to want to work, or have the initiative to do what they need to do or the ability to stick to it. How do we change this condition? We have to put discipline back into the home. "Spare the rod, spoil the child" should become the family motto.

If I tell a my child not to mark on the wall with their crayon and he marks on the wall, and I tell him "I told you not to do that!" Those are just words. They don't mean anything to him. But if he puts a mark on the wall and I take his hand, I'm not saying abuse him, but take a ruler and hit that hand, and when he goes to that wall again he'll look around to see where I'm at. If he does it again and I hit that hand again, the chances are great that he won't do it again and that is what instills the foundation for self-discipline.

Bob Hawkins Owner with loyal sister and Manager Georgia Butler

KEKIONGA BLACKS' War on HIS-Story & Slave Mentality

Lynchology
A Cure for Willie Lynch Enslavement Mentality

Ladies and gentlemen, I would like for you to listen a few moments to the commentary of

Mr. Jihad Shabazz

KEKIONGA BLACKS' War on HIS-Story & Slave Mentality

Hackley Commentary: Since there's strong evidence that all the social, psychological and economic ills facing Fort Wayne and American Black people can be traced back to the dictates of Willie Lynch, **Jihad Shabazz** and I have co-authored a new social history science that we call;

The reason I got on board with the idea of dismantling Willie Lynch is because the climate in this country right now is that many people feel Black people in general, are suffering from a disease called excuse-ism. We make excuses for everything; not succeeding with our families, on our jobs, economically and what have you.

What we have found is for the most part our people do suffer from that. But what is totally unique to American Black people more so than to immigrants who came here in the early part of the 19th Century and who are coming here now is that they have come here with their history in tact. Whereas, our African history was destroyed by the early American Slave owners as they embarked upon a campaign to spiritually break, brainwash and domesticate their African slaves. Therefore we had to find a starting point from which to ascend and we see a workable starting point beginning with Willie Lynch.

Before I go on, yes, there are many other facts, theories and conceptual foundations that could and perhaps should be used to pick apart and destroy slave mentality. Mr. Hackley and I propose our analysis as a starting point. When you and the other detractors propose your theories and remedies on how to mentally emancipate Black people, please submit them to Frost Illustrated. The more Blacks and others we get to think outside the box and start writing, the better it will be for the masses of Black people and the potential enlightenment for all Blacks living in the United States of America.

Now back to our analysis. The Willie Lynch modus operandi was that he devised and implemented a program that would keep slavery perpetual, even when the legalized slavery system was no more. Slave owners could foresee a potential problem when they heard about slave uprisings in Central and South America due to the disproportionate number of Black slaves to White Slave owners. This could cause a problem because within unbalanced numbers, you have a potential powder keg.

So Willie Lynch was brought to the United States to deal with the problem before word had got back to the slaves here in the United States of slaves starting to revolt. He had a program where Africans would be divided through their natural biological differences and he said that this program which began in 1712 would last for 300 years and if it works to its ultimate end, it will last forever.

The reason we're doing this show today is that now, we have a starting point in Fort Wayne. On stage today, we have a lot of people talking about different success stories. I think these stories are the precursors to the dismantling of Willie Lynch and the system that has been put in place today.

Also, the hidden, forgotten and ignored history of Kekionga (Fort Wayne prior to 1794), serves as a precedent for defeating Slave Mentality and White supremacy oriented thinking.

But to recap, many Blacks whose families migrated to Fort Wayne prior too, during and shortly after WWII, went to Harmar School. But most, just like in Anthony Wayne's case, didn't know that he was an Army Brigadier General who was ordered here by George Washington to destroy Kekionga, kill the Indians and burn their crops to starve the Indians they didn't kill during the Winter months. But General Harmar wasn't victorious and because of his historic defeat, he was forced to resign from the American Army in disgrace.

Where are the movies and accolades for and about Chief Little Turtle and the Indians who fought here? Kekionga history does not exist and has become extinct in our modern day mind-set. Our local history has been hidden, making it the perfect precedent for the "Substantial Original Historical Base" that's mentioned in line 10 of the September 22, 2009 Edition of the Final call Newspaper, in the **WARNING: POSSIBLE INTERLOPING NEGA-TIVES** section of the Willie Lynch letter.

The way the Indian Tribal leaders united to fight and momentarily destroy the Euro-American Terrorists with arrows and rifles, conceptually is a direct parallel to show today's Blacks how they can unite and destroy Willie Lynch. The recipe is to substitute the arrows, rifles and knives that were used to kill European Colonialists with testimonials and personal interviews that can kill and destroy the concept of Willie Lynch Slave Mentality. Today we're featuring a wide cross section of Fort Wayne Blacks who have succeeded against the odds through hard work, honesty and perseverance.

One thing I can say about myself in knowing about Willie

Lynch is that when I attended Indiana State University, I met a guy named Omar Farouk. He had wanted to start up a Malcolm X Club there and everyone knows, I am a big fan of Malcolm X. We had speeches during this time in the Nation of Islam about Willie Lynch. In fact, that's when I first heard about Willie Lynch. I never knew the relevance until now as I got older and see how things have taken place in the Black community.

I now understand what Malcolm was talking about. Even though others were starting movements like Martin Luther King, the Willie Lynch story still applied. Those two people, just like I witnessed earlier about Black people not sticking together, I believe that happened between W.E.B. Dubois and Booker T. Washington well as Malcolm X and Martin Luther King. They both had the right programs and were coming closer together, but it never transpired.

So I think with different success stories, different ideologies and knowing Fort Wayne Indian history, we can still dismantle Willie Lynch for the simple fact that we're starting to talk about it. Through this process of dismantling "Lynchology", we can find different solutions that will eventually end the whole concept of perpetual slavery. The reason Mr. Hackley and I coined this "Lynchology" is that we believe it has evolved into a social science.

I was taught back in graduate school about critical theory. My professor talked about a concept called "Epistemology", how do we know what we know. And he discussed a concept called "Ontology" which states ways of knowing, This is the starting point I believe through the different stories from the younger people and older people, these are ways of knowing how to address certain situations, how to persevere and how to dismantle Lynchology.

Through this, we believe there can be a cohesive effort regardless of ideological persuasions that we can go about dismantling Willie Lynch and directly send his ideology into the grave.

Thank you for listening.

You sir~ are a dangerous Subversive

By David Roach

Don't you realize what can happen when the sheeple are jolted from their complacency; and made to think for themselves? Why if people actually started reading, and thinking for themselves, they might start speaking out; and acting like free men of free will.

Heavens to Betsy- are you trying to start a revolution of some kind? Why the very thought of implying that the USA/ white mans government usual modus operandi is the exact same tactics as used by the NAZIS/ THE SOVIETS/ ETC- the holocaust- to conquer; raid; plunder; pillage: and " wink wink CIVILIZE the SAVAGES, HEATHENS, BARBARIANS, UNCONVERTED?

GREAT CAESARS GHOST, MAN!! if word of this gets around, we will have to start questioning our very foundations of governance!! and the legitimacy of our great nation!1 CEASE AND DESIST AT ONCE, before the likes of the TEA PARTY, for example; AND the other lesser educated; ignorant; easily misled low information types get wind of this, we could have a SPARTACIST REVOLT ON OUR HANDS; leading to overturn the statuesque. CHAOS! ANARCHY!! why- exposing the schemers, and their scheming schemes; their heinous conspiracies for global domination- you might as well be painting a target on your back.

But seriously- Eric- you are a scholar, and a gentleman. I was being hyperbolic, and satirical. That's just how I am. I hope you enjoyed the parody, lol.. so my friend, how goes the struggle?

Name Index

Name Index

Name Index